~CODE YOUR OWN

CH

ADVENTURE

By Max Wainewright

QEB

CONTENTS

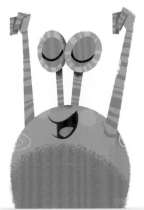
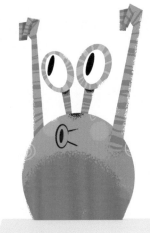

USING SCRATCH

In this book, we will use a computer language called Scratch to code our games. It's free to use and easy to learn. Before you set off on your missions, take a few minutes to get to know Scratch.

FINDING SCRATCH

To start using Scratch, open up a web browser and click in the address bar. Type in **scratch.mit.edu** then press **"Return."** Click **Try it out**.

STARTING SCRATCH

To code a computer game, you need to tell your computer exactly what to do. You do this by giving it commands. In Scratch, commands are shown in the form of "code blocks." You build a game by choosing code blocks and then joining them together to create a program.

Your Scratch screen should look like this:

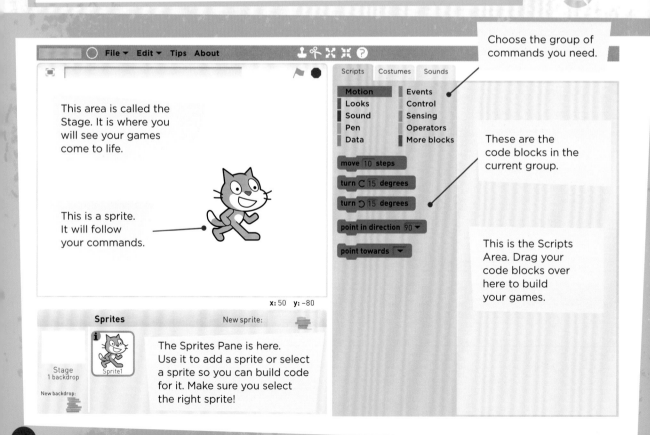

Choose the group of commands you need.

This area is called the Stage. It is where you will see your games come to life.

This is a sprite. It will follow your commands.

These are the code blocks in the current group.

This is the Scripts Area. Drag your code blocks over here to build your games.

The Sprites Pane is here. Use it to add a sprite or select a sprite so you can build code for it. Make sure you select the right sprite!

USING CODE BLOCKS

Before you drag out any code blocks, try clicking on one to make the cat sprite move forward ...

... or rotate 15 degrees.

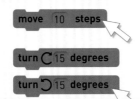

Click in the white boxes (which are shown in this book as colored) then type different numbers to change how far the sprite moves or turns.

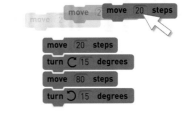

Now try dragging code blocks over to the Scripts Area and joining them together. Click on one of the blocks to run the whole program.

You can break code blocks apart, but you need to start with the bottom block if you want to separate them all. To remove a code block, drag it off the Scripts Area.

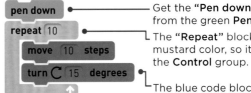

Use the color of the code blocks to figure out which group you will find the block in. It will also give you a clue about what the code block will do.

Get the **"Pen down"** block from the green **Pen** group.

The **"Repeat"** block is a mustard color, so it's in the **Control** group.

The blue code blocks are in the **Motion** group.

USING THE DRAWING AREA

To draw a new sprite, click on the **Paint new sprite** button located in the top bar of the **Sprites Pane**.

To draw a backdrop for the Stage, click on the **Stage** button located in the **Sprites Pane** then click on **Paint new backdrop** underneath it.

The **Drawing Area** will appear on the right of your Scratch screen:

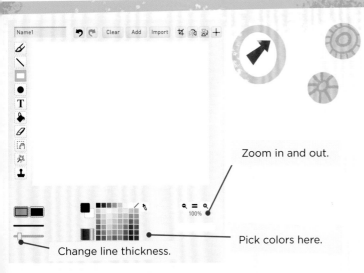

Zoom in and out.

Change line thickness.

Pick colors here.

Brush
Use this tool for drawing.

Rectangle
Draw a rectangle. Hold down the **"Shift"** key to make a square.

Ellipse (Oval)
Draw an ellipse. Hold down the **"Shift"** key to make a circle.

Fill
Fill an area by clicking in it with the mouse.

CODE YOUR OWN SPACE ADVENTURE

A call comes in from Mission Control. Major Kate Glenn is in urgent need of your help. Without a moment's hesitation, you race to Mission Control ...

Thank goodness you are here! An SOS has come in from Planet Zyskinar. They have been invaded by a hostile life form. We need to leave right now!

The problem is that my rocket, the Superlooper, is still in need of repairs after an unlucky asteroid strike on my last mission. I was told you had the skills to help.

Can you help me save the Zyskinarians?

You need to get the Superlooper ready for launch. Draw it on your computer screen and make sure that its rocket blasters are fully functioning!

THE SUPERLOOPER

1. Open **Scratch**.

We need to delete the cat sprite. In the **Sprites Pane**, **right click** the **cat**. On a Mac computer, hold the **"Ctrl"** key then **click**.

Click **Delete**.

2. To start drawing the Superlooper, click the **Paint new sprite** button in the **Sprites Pane**.

3. Now you should be able to see the **Drawing Area**.

Choose the **Ellipse tool.**

At the bottom of the screen, click the **Solid ellipse** so we can draw a filled-in shape.

4. Pick a **dark color** for the rocket fins.

Draw a circle by dragging the mouse. Make it about this size and position in the Drawing Area.

5. Choose a **lighter color**.

Draw a longer ellipse to be the rocket's body.

6. Drag the body so it is in the middle of the circle.

If things go wrong, click **Undo** and go back a step or two.

7. Click the **Select** tool.

Draw a select box around the left side of your artwork.

Press the **"Delete"** key (or **"Backspace"** on a Mac) to delete the selected area.

8. The basic rocket is now ready.

Change color and use the **Ellipse** tool to add portholes.

9. Add any extra details you want using the **Rectangle** tool.

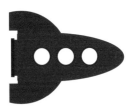

The Superlooper is now ready!

Turn over to find out how to save your Superlooper design so you can use it for the rest of your adventures. Quick—turn over!

Thank you for fixing the Superlooper! We must leave right now to save the Zyskinarians. It's up to you to blast us off into space.
5 – 4 – 3 – 2 – 1 ...

BLAST OFF!

1. Before you do anything else, save the Superlooper rocket sprite you have drawn. This is very important!

In the **Sprites Pane, right click** the Superlooper. On a Mac computer, hold the **"Ctrl"** key and **click**.

Click **Save to local file**.

Type in **Superlooper** as a name for your sprite. Click **OK**.

2. In the middle of the Scratch screen, click the **Scripts** tab so Scratch is ready for you to add some code to make the rocket move.

| Scripts | Costumes |

3. Drag these blocks into the **Scripts Area**, in this order. Remember that the color of each block tells us which group it is in. So the **"When green flag clicked"** block is in the **Events** group. The blue blocks are in the **Motion** group. All the purple blocks are in the **Looks** group. The **"Forever"** loop block is in **Control**.

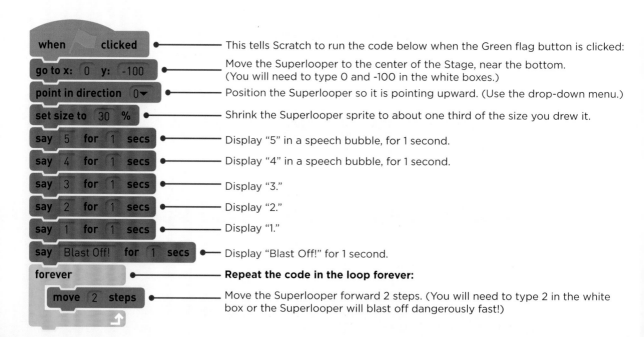

when clicked	This tells Scratch to run the code below when the Green flag button is clicked:
go to x: 0 y: -100	Move the Superlooper to the center of the Stage, near the bottom. (You will need to type 0 and -100 in the white boxes.)
point in direction 0▾	Position the Superlooper so it is pointing upward. (Use the drop-down menu.)
set size to 30 %	Shrink the Superlooper sprite to about one third of the size you drew it.
say 5 for 1 secs	Display "5" in a speech bubble, for 1 second.
say 4 for 1 secs	Display "4" in a speech bubble, for 1 second.
say 3 for 1 secs	Display "3."
say 2 for 1 secs	Display "2."
say 1 for 1 secs	Display "1."
say Blast Off! for 1 secs	Display "Blast Off!" for 1 second.
forever	**Repeat the code in the loop forever:**
move 2 steps	Move the Superlooper forward 2 steps. (You will need to type 2 in the white box or the Superlooper will blast off dangerously fast!)

4. Now we need to set the backdrop for the Stage to show the launch pad area.

In the **Sprites Pane**, click the **Stage** icon.

Below this icon, click on **Choose backdrop from library**.

Choose **Slopes**, then click **OK**.

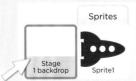

5. Click the **Green flag** button at the top right of the Stage to test your code and launch the Superlooper!

To save your game, click the **File** menu, then **Download to your computer**. When you want to play it again, you can click **File** and **Upload from your computer**.

It is a long journey to Zyskinar. We'll have to take turns piloting the Superlooper. IT'S YOUR TURN NOW!

Take control of the Superlooper. Create code that will make the ship turn to the left and right.

FLY AWAY!

1. Open **Scratch**. Click the **File** menu and **New** to start a new file.

File▼

New

2. We need to delete the cat sprite. In the **Sprites Pane**, **right click** the cat icon. On a Mac computer, hold the **"Ctrl"** key and **click**. Click **Delete**.

duplicate

delete

3. Now we have launched the Superlooper, we need to create a starry sky background.

In the **Sprites Pane**, click the **Stage** icon.

Stage
1 backdrop

Just below, click **Choose backdrop from library**.

Choose **Stars**, then click **OK**.

Backdrop Library

Stars

4. Now you need to upload the Superlooper sprite that you drew earlier. (If you haven't already drawn the Superlooper, turn to page 7 and follow steps 2 to 9 now.)

In the **Sprites Pane**, click **Upload sprite from file**.

Find your file and click **OK**.

5.

Scripts

Now you need to add code to make the Superlooper fly upward.

In the center of the screen, click the **Scripts** tab. Drag this code into the **Scripts Area**. Remember to look for each block in the code group with the right color.

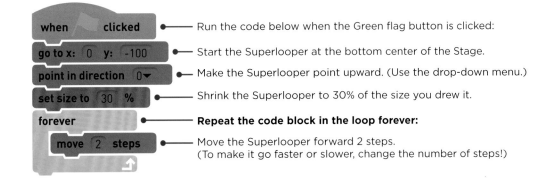

when [flag] clicked ●—— Run the code below when the Green flag button is clicked:

go to x: 0 y: -100 ●—— Start the Superlooper at the bottom center of the Stage.

point in direction 0▼ ●—— Make the Superlooper point upward. (Use the drop-down menu.)

set size to 30 % ●—— Shrink the Superlooper to 30% of the size you drew it.

forever ●——— **Repeat the code block in the loop forever:**

move 2 steps ●—— Move the Superlooper forward 2 steps.
(To make it go faster or slower, change the number of steps!)

---

6. Add these two separate blocks of code to make the Superlooper turn left or right when you press the cursor keys on your keyboard.

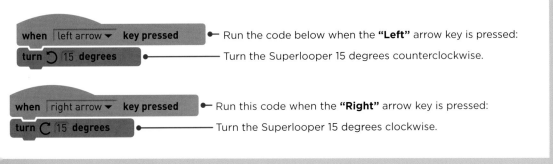

when [left arrow ▼] key pressed ●— Run the code below when the **"Left"** arrow key is pressed:

turn ↺ 15 degrees ●——— Turn the Superlooper 15 degrees counterclockwise.

when [right arrow ▼] key pressed ●— Run this code when the **"Right"** arrow key is pressed:

turn ↻ 15 degrees ●——— Turn the Superlooper 15 degrees clockwise.

---

7. Click the **Green flag** button at the top right of the Stage to test your code. Practice flying around space to prepare yourself for the next part of your mission.

Click the **File** menu then **Download to your computer** if you want to save this game.

We've hit a radiation field! We must swerve to avoid the dangerous yellow particles or we'll be blown to smithereens!

Quick! You need to create code to make the Superlooper avoid the yellow particles.

RADIATION FIELD

1. Open **Scratch**. Start a new file.

New

2. **Right click** the cat sprite. On a Mac, hold **"Ctrl"** and **click**. Click **Delete**.

3.

To draw the radiation field, click the **Backdrops** tab.

Scripts | Backdrops

Now you can see the **Drawing Area**. Choose the **Fill** tool.

Choose **black**.

Fill in the background by clicking on it.

4.

Now choose the **Brush** tool.

Choose **yellow**.

Make the brush width thicker.

Use the brush to draw in the dangerous yellow particles in the radiation field. Do not add so many dots that the Superlooper will never be able to pass through them.

5. Now you need to upload the Superlooper sprite that you drew earlier. In the **Sprites Pane**, click **Upload sprite from file**. Find your file and click **OK**. (If you haven't already drawn the Superlooper, turn to page 7 and follow steps 2 to 9 now.)

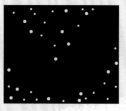

My Documents

game.sb2
maze.sb2
Superlooper.sprite2

OK

6. Let's add a sound effect to play when the rocket hits the radiation field.

Choose the **Sounds** tab.

Click the **Choose sound from library** button.

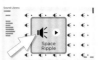

Scroll down to choose **Space ripple**. Click **OK**.

7.

Click the **Scripts** tab. Add all this code to make the rocket move until it hits a dangerous yellow particle. The **"Touching color"** block is in the **Sensing** group. Drop it into the hole in the **"Repeat until"** loop.

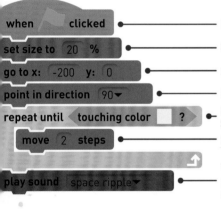

Run the code when the Green flag is clicked:

Shrink the Superlooper to 20% of its size.

Start at the left side of the Stage.

Point the Superlooper to the right.

Repeat the code in the loop until the Superlooper hits a yellow particle:

Move the rocket forward 2 steps.

When the Superlooper hits a yellow particle, play a sound effect. (Choose Space ripple using the drop-down menu.)

How to set the color for a "Touching" block

Click the color square.

touching color ?

The pointer changes.

On the Stage, click the color you want to check for.

The color is set.

touching color ?

8. Add this code to steer the rocket. See page 11 step 6 for help in understanding how this code works.

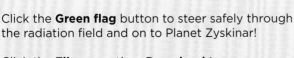

 Click the **Green flag** button to steer safely through the radiation field and on to Planet Zyskinar!

Click the **File** menu then **Download to your computer** to save this game.

Phew! You made it through the radiation field and are now within two light years of Planet Zyksinar. But Kate has bad news ...

It's one crisis after another! The scanners tell me we are entering an asteroid field. Blast those rocks with the ship's lasers ...

Now figure out how to build code to swerve the Superlooper smoothly out of the way of any oncoming asteroids. And don't forget to code a laser sprite that you can fire at that asteroid sprite.

ASTEROID ATTACK

1. Open **Scratch**. Start a new file.

File▾

New

2. **Right click** the cat sprite. On a Mac, hold **"Ctrl"** and **click**. Click **Delete**.

duplicate

delete

3. Now we will create a starry background.

In the **Sprites Pane**, click the **Stage** icon.

Stage
1 backdrop

Just below, click **Choose backdrop from library**.

Choose **Stars**, then click **OK**.

Backdrop Library

Stars

4. Now you need to upload the Superlooper sprite that you drew earlier. In the **Sprites Pane**, click **Upload sprite from file**. Find your file and click **OK**. (If you haven't already drawn the Superlooper, turn to page 7 and follow steps 2 to 9 now.)

```
My Documents

game.sb2
maze.sb2
Superlooper.sprite2
                    OK
```

5. Click the **Scripts** tab and drag this code over to the **Scripts Area**. Make sure that the **Superlooper** is selected in the **Sprites Pane**. The **"Key pressed?"** blocks are in the **Sensing** group. You will need to drop them into the holes in the **"If then"** loop blocks.

Scripts

when clicked	Run this code when the Green flag button is clicked:
go to x: 0 y: 0	Move the Superlooper to the center of the Stage.
set size to 35 %	Shrink the Superlooper to 35% of its size.
forever	**Repeat the code in the loop forever:**
if key left arrow pressed? then	**If the "Left" cursor key is pressed, run this code:**
turn ↺ 5 degrees	Turn the Superlooper 5 degrees counterclockwise. (Type 5 into the white box.)
if key right arrow pressed? then	**If the "Right" cursor key is pressed, run this code:**
turn ↻ 5 degrees	Turn the Superlooper 5 degrees clockwise.

6. Click the **Green flag** button to test your code so far. The Superlooper should turn when you press the arrow keys on your keyboard. The ship will need to be easy to maneuver once the asteroids start coming ...

7. Now we will create a sprite to use as our laser. In the **Sprites Pane**, click the **Choose sprite from library** button.

Click the **Button 1** icon.

Sprite Library

Button1

Click **OK**.

OK

15

8. Click the **Scripts** tab and add this code for the laser (Button1) sprite.

Scripts

```
when [green flag] clicked
set size to (10) %
```
— Run the code below when the Green flag button is clicked:
— Shrink the laser sprite to 10% of its size.

★

```
when [space ▾] key pressed
go to x: (0) y: (0)
point in direction (direction ▾ of Sprite1 ▾)
repeat until < touching [edge ▾] ? >
    move (10) steps
```
— When the **"Space"** key is pressed, run this code:
— Move the laser to the center of the Stage.
— Point the laser in the direction of the Superlooper.
Repeat the code in the loop until the laser reaches the edge of the screen:
— Move the laser forward 10 steps.

★ ★ ★ ★

Need help finding this code block?

`direction ▾ of Sprite1 ▾`

| **Sensing**

Choose the **Sensing** group.

`x position ▾ of Button1 ▾`

Near the bottom of the group, find this block.

`point in direction 10 ▾` `x position ▾ of Button1 ▾`

Dragging by the left corner, drop it in the hole in the **"Point in direction"** block.

direction ▾ / x position / y position / direction

Sprite1 ▾ / Stage / Sprite1

Use the menus to choose **Direction** and **Sprite1**.

9. Test your code so far. You should still be able to turn the Superlooper left and right. Try pressing the **"Space"** bar on your keyboard to fire the laser.

10. Now we need to draw an asteroid.

Click the **Paint new sprite** icon.

50%

Make your asteroid about **half the height** of the Drawing Area. If it is very different from this size, the game won't work properly.

Choose the **Ellipse** tool.

Set it to solid fill.

Choose a suitable asteroid color.

Draw a circle.

Use the **Eraser** to make craters.

Use the **Eraser** to make the edges rougher.

Use **Undo** if you make a mistake.

11. Let's add a sound effect that will play when the laser hits the asteroid.

Click on the
Sounds tab.

Click **Choose
sound from
library**.

New sound:

Scroll down and
choose the
Zoop sound.

Click **OK**.

12. Click the **Scripts** tab and drag this code over to the **Scripts Area** for the asteroid.   Scripts

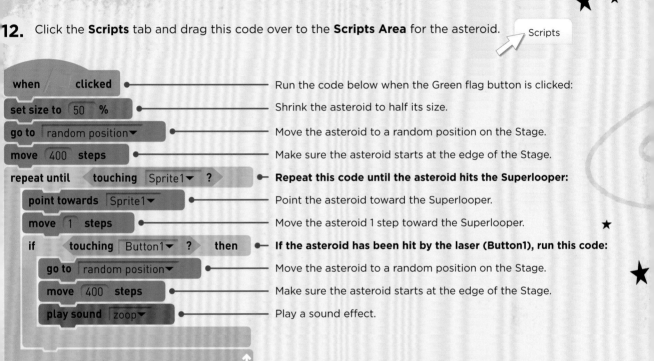

when clicked — Run the code below when the Green flag button is clicked:

set size to 50 % — Shrink the asteroid to half its size.

go to random position — Move the asteroid to a random position on the Stage.

move 400 steps — Make sure the asteroid starts at the edge of the Stage.

repeat until touching Sprite1 ? — **Repeat this code until the asteroid hits the Superlooper:**

point towards Sprite1 — Point the asteroid toward the Superlooper.

move 1 steps — Move the asteroid 1 step toward the Superlooper.

if touching Button1 ? then — **If the asteroid has been hit by the laser (Button1), run this code:**

go to random position — Move the asteroid to a random position on the Stage.

move 400 steps — Make sure the asteroid starts at the edge of the Stage.

play sound zoop — Play a sound effect.

stop all — If the asteroid hits the Superlooper, stop all the other code,
so the laser stops and the Superlooper can't turn.

13. Press the **Green flag** button to
defend the Superlooper against
the asteroids. Your game should
look like this!

To save your game, choose **File**
and **Download to your computer**.

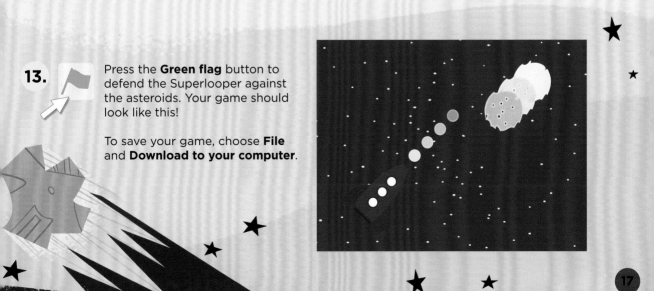

OH NO! Those asteroids bashed holes in the Superlooper. All our food supplies have floated out into space!

I need you to go on a space walk to repair the hull. And don't forget to collect the floating food ...

You need to build code that allows you to collect the bananas that are floating around the Superlooper. You also need to fix the damage to the hull. That's easier than it sounds—you can "fix" the holes by touching them! First of all, draw yourself a space suit and jet pack.

SPACE WALK!

1. Open **Scratch**. Start a new file.

File ▼

New

2. **Right click** the cat sprite. On a Mac, hold **"Ctrl"** and **click**.

duplicate
delete

Click **Delete**.

3. Now we will create a starry background.

Stage
1 backdrop

In the **Sprites Pane**, click the **Stage** icon.

Just below, click **Choose backdrop from library**.

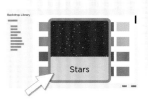
Backdrop Library
Stars

Choose **Stars**, then click **OK**.

4. Upload your **Superlooper** sprite.

5. In the Scratch **Menu bar**, click the **Grow** button. Now click one or more times on the **Superlooper** on the **Stage**. Make it grow until it is about **half** the width of the Stage.

6. We need to draw your space suit and jet pack.

While drawing, keep in mind that the astronaut sprite needs to be about a **third of the width** of the Drawing Area. If it's much bigger or smaller than this size, the game will not work properly.

33%

In the **Sprites Pane**, click the **Paint new sprite** icon.

Choose the **Rectangle** tool to start with.

Make sure it is set to fill in.

If you make a mistake, just click **Undo**.

Use three **white** rectangles to draw your space suit.

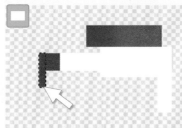

Use **dark gray** to draw your boots and jet pack.

Use **light gray** for your gloves and collar.

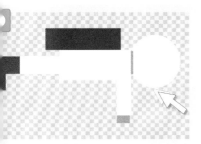

Now choose the **Ellipse** tool to draw your helmet.

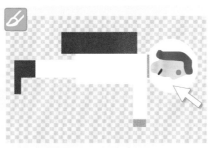

Use the **Brush** tool and pick colors to draw your face inside the helmet.

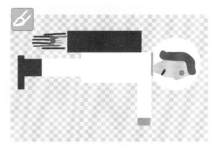

Finally, draw some flames coming from your jet pack.

7. Now click the **Scripts** tab and drag this code to the **Scripts Area** to make the jet pack zoom you around space. Make sure you have the **astronaut** icon selected in the **Sprites Pane**.

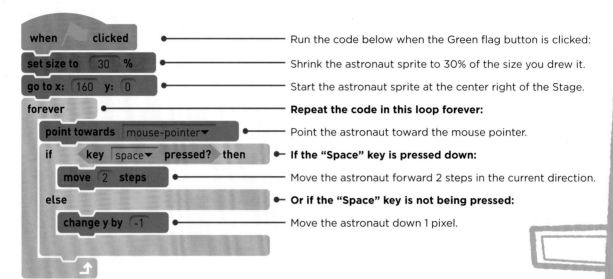

when clicked	Run the code below when the Green flag button is clicked:
set size to 30 %	Shrink the astronaut sprite to 30% of the size you drew it.
go to x: 160 y: 0	Start the astronaut sprite at the center right of the Stage.
forever	**Repeat the code in this loop forever:**
point towards mouse-pointer▼	Point the astronaut toward the mouse pointer.
if key space▼ pressed? then	**If the "Space" key is pressed down:**
move 2 steps	Move the astronaut forward 2 steps in the current direction.
else	**Or if the "Space" key is not being pressed:**
change y by -1	Move the astronaut down 1 pixel.

Click the **Green flag** button to try flying around. Press the **"Space"** bar to fire the jet pack, and use the **mouse** to point where you want to fly.

8. Now we will add the floating food.

In the **Sprites Pane**, click **Choose sprite from library**.

Click the **Bananas** icon.

Click **OK**.

9. Click the **Scripts** tab and add this code for the **bananas** sprite.

when clicked	Run the code below when the Green flag button is clicked:
set size to 30 %	Shrink the bananas to 30% of their size.
show	Make sure the bananas are visible on the Stage.
repeat until touching Sprite2▼ ?	**Repeat the code in the loop until the bananas have been touched by Sprite2 (the astronaut):**
turn ↺ 5▼ degrees	Rotate the bananas 5 degrees counterclockwise.
hide	Hide the bananas—they have been grabbed by the astronaut!

10. We need to draw the damage to the Superlooper as a new sprite, so click **Paint new sprite**.

Use the **Line** tool to start drawing a damaged section of the Superlooper in **pale gray**.

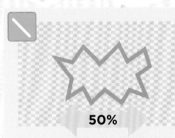

50%

Make sure you join the lines up. Your shape should be about **half the width** of the Drawing Area.

Use the **Fill** tool to color in the damage shape.

11. Click the **Scripts** tab and add this code for the **damage** sprite. To create the sound effect **Computer beeps**, turn to page 17 and follow step 11. The sound effect isn't vital, but it's fun!

Scripts

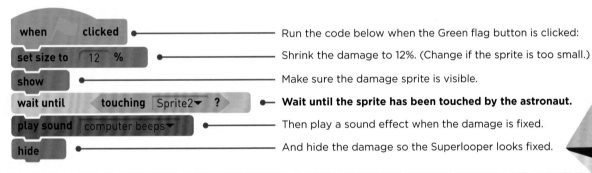

when [green flag] clicked	Run the code below when the Green flag button is clicked:
set size to 12 %	Shrink the damage to 12%. (Change if the sprite is too small.)
show	Make sure the damage sprite is visible.
wait until < touching Sprite2 ? >	**Wait until the sprite has been touched by the astronaut.**
play sound computer beeps	Then play a sound effect when the damage is fixed.
hide	And hide the damage so the Superlooper looks fixed.

12. In the Sprites Pane, **right click** the **banana** sprite and choose **Duplicate**. Duplicate three more.

Drag the duplicates around the screen.

13. **Right click** the **damage** sprite and choose **Duplicate**. Duplicate three more.

Drag the duplicates over the Superlooper rocket.

14. Now click the **Green flag** button to collect the bananas and repair the Superlooper!

Save your game by choosing **File** then **Download to your computer**.

At last! You touch down on the barren surface of Planet Zyskinar. You cannot see any Zyskinarians through the porthole, but ...

Planet Zyskinar has been invaded by giant bugs! Zyskinar used to be a beautiful place, covered in fruit trees and flowers. The bugs have eaten everything in sight! The Zyskinarians must be hiding somewhere. We must save the planet! But how?

You wrack your brains to come up with a clever plan. That's it! If the bugs like fruit so much, you can lure them into the Superlooper's cargo hold with those bananas you collected earlier. Make sure you add code to count how many bugs you catch.

GOING BANANAS

1. Start a new Scratch file. **Delete** the **cat sprite**.

2. We will create a background showing the barren surface of Planet Zyskinar.

Click the **Stage** icon.

Just below, click **Choose backdrop from library**.

Choose **Moon**, then click **OK**.

3. We want to fill the Stage with the surface of the planet, so we need to stretch part of the image.

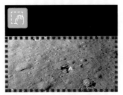

Choose the **Select** tool. Drag a box around the bottom half of the image.

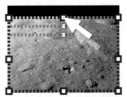

Move your mouse over the handle at the top. Drag it up to stretch the picture.

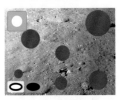

Choose the **Ellipse** tool and set it to solid fill. Draw **brown** craters.

4. Upload your **Superlooper** sprite.

5. Click the **Shrink** button in the **Menu bar**. Now click the **Superlooper** on the Stage to shrink it until it is about the size of one of the craters.

6. To create a banana sprite, click the **Choose sprite from library** button.

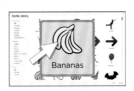

Click the **Bananas** icon.

Click **OK**.

7. We need a way to count how many bugs have been lured away. We will use a special part of our program to do this, called a variable. Variables are a way of storing numbers to keep score.

Sound
Pen
Data

Click the **Data** group.

Make a Variable

Click **Make a variable**.

Variable name: bugs

Call it **bugs**.

OK

Then click **OK**.

8. Now add code for the **bananas** sprite so you can make it follow the mouse around the Stage—and use it to lure the bugs back to your spaceship! The orange blocks are in the **Data** group. The green **"Equals"** block is in the **Operators** group. You will need to drop the little **"Bugs"** block into its left-hand hole.

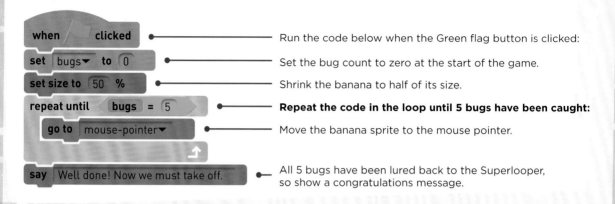

when clicked	Run the code below when the Green flag button is clicked:
set bugs▼ **to** 0	Set the bug count to zero at the start of the game.
set size to 50 %	Shrink the banana to half of its size.
repeat until bugs = 5	**Repeat the code in the loop until 5 bugs have been caught:**
go to mouse-pointer▼	Move the banana sprite to the mouse pointer.
say Well done! Now we must take off.	All 5 bugs have been lured back to the Superlooper, so show a congratulations message.

9. Now we need to create those hungry giant bugs! Click **Choose sprite from library**.

Click the **Beetle** icon.

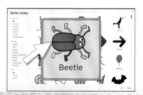

Beetle

Click **OK**.

OK

10. Click the **Scripts** tab and add this code to the **bug** to make it follow the banana.

Scripts

when clicked	Run the code below when the Green flag button is clicked:
show	Make sure the bug is visible.
set size to 40 %	Shrink the bug to 40% of its size.
go to random position▼	Start it in a random place on the Stage.
repeat until touching Sprite1▼ ?	**Repeat the code in the loop until the bug touches the Superlooper:**
point towards mouse-pointer▼	Point the bug toward the mouse pointer (the banana will be there).
move 1 **steps**	Move the bug forward 1 step.
if touching color ? **then**	**If the banana is touching a brown crater (see page 13 for help setting the color to brown), then run this code:**
move -2 **steps**	Move the bug backward 2 steps.
change bugs▼ **by** 1	Increase the bug count by 1.
hide	Hide the bug—it is now in the Superlooper!

11. We need 4 more bugs to finish off our game.

In the **Sprites Pane**, **right click** the bug. On a Mac, hold **"Ctrl"** and **click**. Click **Duplicate**. Repeat this 3 more times. Drag the bugs around the Stage.

Click the **Green flag** to lure the giant bugs into the Superlooper.

To save your game, click **File** and **Download to your computer**.

The giant bugs are now all safely inside the Superlooper's cargo hold. They waste no time in eating up the remaining bananas!

You set out on foot in search of the Zyskinarians. **Suddenly one pops out of a hole!**

Help! My fellow Zyskinarians are hiding in tunnels deep beneath the ground. They are running out of air. I beg you to rescue them in your spaceship before it is too late.

You must fly the Superlooper through the tunnels to rescue the Zyskinarians. It will be tricky squeezing through those tight gaps. But you must act quickly!

UNDERGROUND RESCUE

1. Start a new Scratch file.

Delete the **cat sprite**.

2. To draw a backdrop showing the Planet Zyskinar and its underground tunnels, click the **Backdrops** tab. Now you should be able to see the **Drawing Area**.

Backdrops

Use the **Fill** tool to color the background **black**, then use a **white Brush** to add stars at the top.

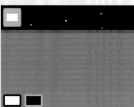

Draw a large **pale brown** rectangle and a thin, **darker** one at the top.

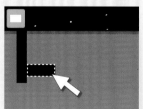

Draw **black** rectangles to create tunnels. Make them roughly the width shown here.

Use the **Brush** tool to add some texture to the ground.

3. **Upload** your **Superlooper** sprite.

4. Let's animate the Superlooper's engine so it looks as if it is blasting. To do this we will create a second "costume" for the Superlooper, showing flames coming from the engine. We will tell Scratch to switch to the second costume when the Superlooper is flying along.

In the center of the Scratch screen, click the **Costumes** tab, then **right click** the **Superlooper** icon. On a Mac, hold **"Ctrl"** and **click**.

Costume1
464x265

Costume2
464x265

The Superlooper sprite now has two costumes.

5. Make sure you have **costume2** selected. On the **Drawing Area**, use the **Brush** tool to draw short flames coming from the engine.

To get a preview of your animation, click on the costume1 icon, then costume2, then costume1 ... It should look as if the flames are flickering.

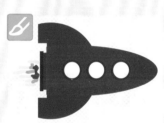

6. Scripts

Click the **Scripts** tab and add this code to the Superlooper to make it fly around.

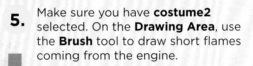

Add these 4 separate sets of code, one for each direction: up, down, left, and right.

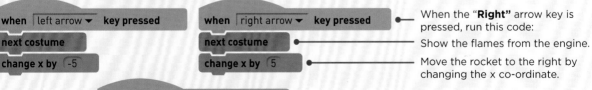

When the "**Right**" arrow key is pressed, run this code:

Show the flames from the engine.

Move the rocket to the right by changing the x co-ordinate.

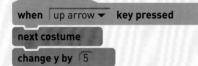

If you haven't learned about co-ordinates yet, don't worry—this is a good way to find out about them. Just test out what these 4 sets of blocks do!

7. We need to make a variable to count how many Zyskinarians have been saved.
Remember: a variable is the way we keep score in a computer program.

Sound
Pen
Data

Make a Variable

Variable name: saved

OK

Click the **Data** group.   Click **Make a variable**.   Call it **saved**.   Then click **OK**.

8. Now click the **Scripts** tab and add this code to the **Superlooper**.

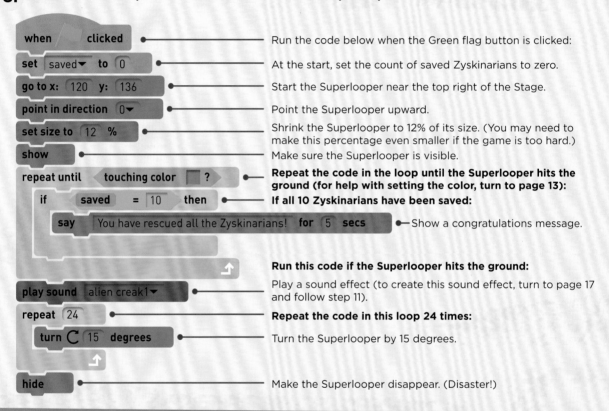

when ⚑ clicked ● ──────────── Run the code below when the Green flag button is clicked:

set saved▾ to 0 ● ──────────── At the start, set the count of saved Zyskinarians to zero.

go to x: 120 y: 136 ● ──────────── Start the Superlooper near the top right of the Stage.

point in direction 0▾ ● ──────────── Point the Superlooper upward.

set size to 12 % ● ──────────── Shrink the Superlooper to 12% of its size. (You may need to make this percentage even smaller if the game is too hard.)

show ● ──────────── Make sure the Superlooper is visible.

repeat until touching color ☐ ? ● ──────────── **Repeat the code in the loop until the Superlooper hits the ground (for help with setting the color, turn to page 13):**

if saved = 10 then ● ──────────── **If all 10 Zyskinarians have been saved:**

say You have rescued all the Zyskinarians! for 5 secs ●─── Show a congratulations message.

Run this code if the Superlooper hits the ground:

play sound alien creak1▾ ● ──────────── Play a sound effect (to create this sound effect, turn to page 17 and follow step 11).

repeat 24 ● ──────────── **Repeat the code in this loop 24 times:**

turn ↻ 15 degrees ● ──────────── Turn the Superlooper by 15 degrees.

hide ● ──────────── Make the Superlooper disappear. (Disaster!)

9. Of course, we need to draw a Zyskinarian sprite! Click the **Paint new sprite** icon.

 Make your Zyskinarian about **half the height** of the Drawing Area.

Use the **Brush** tool.

Make the brush quite thick.

Design your own Zyskinarian.

 Use the **Undo** button if you're not happy with what you've drawn.

10. Click the **Shrink** button.
Now **click** the **Zyskinarian** on the **Stage** until it fits inside one of the tunnels.

11. Click the **Scripts** tab and add this code to the **Zyskinarian**.
Make sure you have your Zyskinarian selected.

Scripts

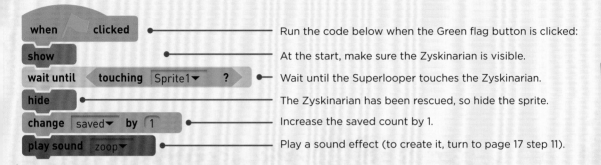

when ⚑ clicked	Run the code below when the Green flag button is clicked:
show	At the start, make sure the Zyskinarian is visible.
wait until ⟨ touching Sprite1▼ ? ⟩	Wait until the Superlooper touches the Zyskinarian.
hide	The Zyskinarian has been rescued, so hide the sprite.
change saved▼ by 1	Increase the saved count by 1.
play sound zoop▼	Play a sound effect (to create it, turn to page 17 step 11).

12. To create 9 more Zyskinarians (there aren't many of them on the planet!), **right click** the **Zyskinarian** icon in the **Sprites Pane**. On a Mac, hold **"Ctrl"** and **click**. Choose **Duplicate**.

Duplicate another 8 so there are 10 altogether.

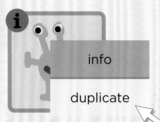

info

duplicate

Drag the Zyskinarians into their hiding places in the tunnels.

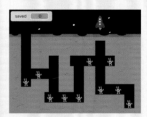

 Now race to rescue the Zyskinarians before they run out of air!
To save your game, choose **File** then **Download to your computer**.

THANK YOU!

THANK YOU!

YOU SAVED US!

You still need to get rid of those giant bugs that are munching bananas in the Superlooper's cargo hold. Help Astronaut Kate fly the bugs back to their home world, the planet Bananareeta.

FLIGHT TO BANANAREETA

1. Start a new Scratch file and **delete** the **cat sprite**.

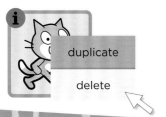

2. Now we will create a background for the Superlooper's takeoff from Planet Zyskinar. Click the **Backdrops** tab. Now you should be able to see the **Drawing Area**.

Use the **Fill** tool to color the background **black**, then use a **white Brush** to add stars.

Draw a wide **pale brown** rectangle and a thin, **darker** one at the top.

3. To create the planet Bananareeta, click **Choose sprite from library**.

Click the **Beachball** icon.

Click **OK**.

4. Click the **Scripts** tab and add this code to **Bananareeta** (the beachball sprite).

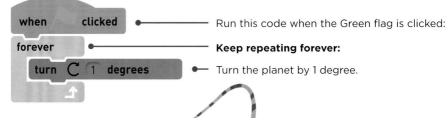

Run this code when the Green flag is clicked:

Keep repeating forever:

Turn the planet by 1 degree.

5. **Upload** your **Superlooper** sprite.

6.

Scripts

Click the **Scripts** tab and add this code to the **Superlooper**.

```
when ⚑ clicked
```
Run this code when the Green flag is clicked:

```
go to x: 0 y: -120
```
Start the Superlooper at the bottom.

```
set size to 12 %
```
Shrink the Superlooper to 12% of its size.

```
point in direction 0▼
```
Make the Superlooper point upward.

```
repeat until    touching Beachball▼ ?
```
Repeat until the Superlooper reaches Bananareeta.

```
   move 1 steps
```
Move the Superlooper 1 step forward.

```
when left arrow ▼ key pressed
```
Run this code when the **"Left"** arrow key is pressed:

```
turn ↺ 3 degrees
```
Turn the Superlooper 3 degrees counterclockwise.

```
when right arrow ▼ key pressed
```
Run this code when the **"Right"** arrow key is pressed:

```
turn ↻ 3 degrees
```
Turn the Superlooper 3 degrees clockwise.

Click the **Green flag** to fly the Superlooper and its cargo to Bananareeta. Try orbiting the planet before landing.

Thank you! Without your help I could never have saved Planet Zyskinar. Our mission was a great success. It's time to fly home to Earth!

31

CODE YOUR OWN PIRATE ADVENTURE

You receive a message in a bottle from your old friend Pirate Pierre. It asks you to meet Pierre at the Smuggler's Inn...

You've come at last, matey. Those terrrrrible ghost pirates have been up to their old tricks! Those long dead scallywags have stolen my treasure. You must help me catch 'em on board my good ship, the *Jolly Coder*.

But shiver me timbers, you look like a landlubber! You can't set foot on board dressed like that!

Pirate Pierre is right. Before you go any further, you must disguise yourself as a pirate.

PIRATE AHOY!

1. Open **Scratch**.

First, we need to delete the cat sprite. In the **Sprites Pane**, **right click** the **cat**. On a Mac, hold the "Ctrl" key then **click**.

Click **Delete**.

2. To start drawing yourself, click the **Paint new sprite** button in the **Sprites Pane**.

3. Now you should be able to see the **Drawing Area**.

 Choose the **Ellipse** tool.

 At the bottom of the screen, click the **Solid ellipse** so we can draw a filled-in shape.

4. Select a skin color.

Draw a circle for your head by dragging the mouse in the top center of the Drawing Area.

5. Now choose the **Rectangle** tool.

50%

Draw two red rectangles. Make sure your pirate is about **half the width** of the Drawing Area. If not, your games might not work.

6. Use rectangles to make pants and boots.

 If things go wrong, click **Undo** and go back a step or two.

7.  Add some stripes to your shirt.

8. Use the **Brush** tool to draw your hat.

Use thin lines for the details.

Make the lines thicker.

Pick **white** for the skull and crossbones.

9. Use the **Brush** tool to add any last details...   ...and make the outfit your own.

Now turn over to find out how to save your pirate drawing so you can use it on your voyage!

POLLY THE PARROT

Wait, shipmate. We can't set sail without Polly the Parrot. Go to the docks and find her!

1. Before you do anything else, save the pirate sprite you drew on page 33. This means you will be able to load the pirate sprite into other games and activities that you code.

In the **Sprites Pane**, **right click** your pirate. On a Mac, hold **"Ctrl"** and **click**.

Click **Save to local file**.

Type in **pirate** as a name for your sprite and click **OK**.

2. In the middle of the Scratch screen, click the **Scripts** tab so Scratch is ready for you to add some code to make your pirate move.

Scripts

3. Drag these blocks into the **Scripts Area**, in this order. Remember that the color of each block tells us which group it is in. So the **"When green flag clicked"** block is in the **Events** group. The blue blocks are in the **Motion** group. All the purple blocks are in the **Looks** group. The **"Repeat"** loop block is in **Control**. You can click in the white box in a block to change the message or number, so click in the **"Say"** block to type in **"Ahoy there, Polly!"**

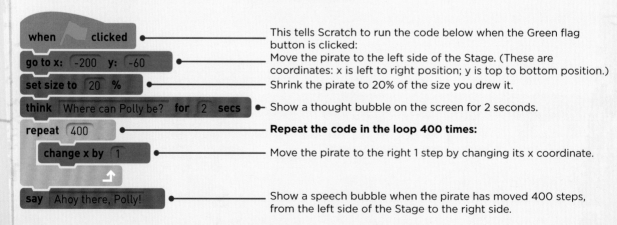

when [flag] clicked • — This tells Scratch to run the code below when the Green flag button is clicked:

go to x: -200 y: -60 • — Move the pirate to the left side of the Stage. (These are coordinates: x is left to right position; y is top to bottom position.)

set size to 20 % • — Shrink the pirate to 20% of the size you drew it.

think Where can Polly be? for 2 secs • — Show a thought bubble on the screen for 2 seconds.

repeat 400 • — **Repeat the code in the loop 400 times:**

change x by 1 • — Move the pirate to the right 1 step by changing its x coordinate.

say Ahoy there, Polly! • — Show a speech bubble when the pirate has moved 400 steps, from the left side of the Stage to the right side.

34

4. Set the background for the Stage to show the docks.

In the **Sprites Pane**, click the **Stage** icon.

Just below, click on **Choose backdrop from library**.

Choose **Boardwalk** then click **OK**.

5. To create Polly the Parrot, click the **Choose sprite from library** button in the **Sprites Pane**.

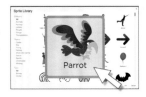

Scroll down then click the **Parrot** image.

Click **OK**.

Click on the **Stage** and drag Polly the Parrot all the way over to the **right-hand side**.

6. Click the **Green flag** button at the top right of the Stage to test your code. What happens when you find Polly?

To save your game, click the **File** menu, then **Download to your computer**. Then to play it again, you can click **File** and **Upload from your computer**.

Pretty Polly! Pretty Polly!

Pirate Pierre welcomes you aboard the *Jolly Coder*...

Those filthy seadogs have damaged my beautiful ship as well as stolen my treasure! Before we head to sea, we need to fix 'er. Shake a leg, me ol' matey!

Filthy seadogs!

Help Pirate Pierre fix the *Jolly Coder* by drawing a seaworthy pirate ship.

THE JOLLY CODER

1. Start a new Scratch file by clicking **File** then **New**.

In the **Sprites Pane**, **right click** the **cat**. On a Mac computer, hold the **"Ctrl"** key then **click**.

Click **Delete**.

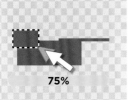

2. Start drawing your ship by clicking the **Paint new sprite** button.

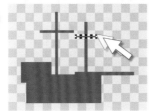

3. Choose the **Rectangle** tool.

At the bottom of the screen, click the **Solid rectangle**.

Select a **dark brown**.

4. Start with three rectangles.

75%

Make sure your drawing is about **three-quarters of the width** of the Drawing Area.

If not, your games may not work. Click **Undo** and try again if you need to.

5.

Draw four thin rectangles to make the masts.

6.

Draw three white sails and one black one.

7.

Use a thick **Brush** to round the front.

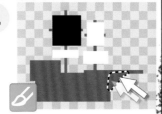

8.

Using the **Brush**, draw the skull and crossbones flag and some portholes.

9.

Use the **Eraser** to smooth the bottom of the ship.

10.

Use the **Rectangle** to add details in **dark brown**.

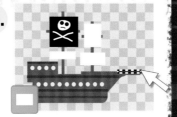

11.

In the **Sprites Pane**, **right click** the **Jolly Coder** sprite. On a Mac, hold **"Ctrl"** and **click**. Choose **Save to local file** so that you can use your ship later. Call your sprite **jollycoder**.

Thankee, shipmate. Away
we go! Take the wheel and
we'll soon chase down those
ghostly scallywags.

Ghostly
scallywags!

Now you need to create
code to sail the *Jolly Coder*
across the waves.

SAIL AWAY

1. File▼   Start a
New   new file.

2. **Right click** the **cat**. On a Mac, hold **"Ctrl"** and **click**.

duplicate

delete

Choose
Delete.

3. In the **Sprites Pane**,
click **Upload sprite
from file**.

My Documents

game.sb2
maze.sb2
jollycoder.sprite2

OK

Find your
jollycoder
sprite and
click **OK**.

The sprite
will appear
in the Sprites
Pane.

Sprite1

4. In the center of the screen, click the **Scripts** tab and drag this code into the **Scripts Area**.

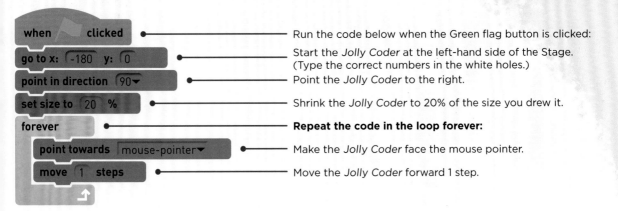

when 🚩 clicked	Run the code below when the Green flag button is clicked:
go to x: -180 y: 0	Start the *Jolly Coder* at the left-hand side of the Stage. (Type the correct numbers in the white holes.)
point in direction 90▾	Point the *Jolly Coder* to the right.
set size to 20 %	Shrink the *Jolly Coder* to 20% of the size you drew it.
forever	**Repeat the code in the loop forever:**
point towards mouse-pointer▾	Make the *Jolly Coder* face the mouse pointer.
move 1 steps	Move the *Jolly Coder* forward 1 step.

5. Now we will create a sea background.

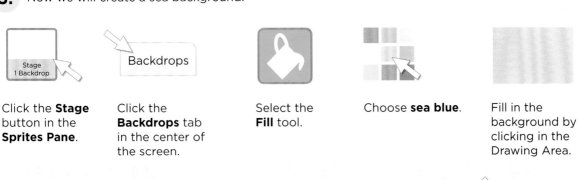

Click the **Stage** button in the **Sprites Pane**.

Click the **Backdrops** tab in the center of the screen.

Select the **Fill** tool.

Choose **sea blue**.

Fill in the background by clicking in the Drawing Area.

6. Click the **Green flag** button at the top right of the Stage to test your code. Practice sailing around. Move your mouse pointer to make the *Jolly Coder* sail toward it.

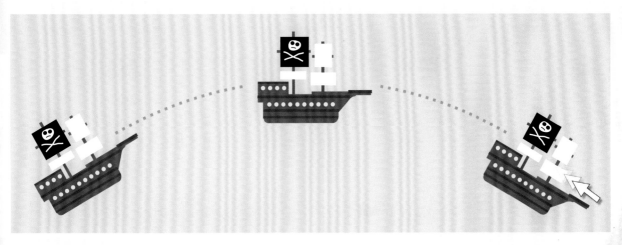

7. To save this part of your adventure, click the **File** menu then **Download to your computer**.

If I know those ghost pirates, they'll have buried my treasure in their old hang-out—Haunted Island!

WATCH THE ROCKS

Head east to reach Haunted Island.
But watch out—don't run aground on those rocks!

1. Start a new file.

File ▾

New

2. **Right click** the **cat**. On a Mac, hold **"Ctrl"** and **click**.

duplicate

delete

Choose **Delete**.

3. Backdrops

Click the **Backdrops** tab.

Choose the **Fill** tool.

Choose **sea blue**.

Fill in the background.

4.

Choose the **Brush** tool.

Choose **black**.

Make the brush width **thicker**.

Use the brush to draw outlines of rocks.

5.

Choose the **Fill** tool.

Fill in the rocks by clicking inside them.

If the color leaks out of the rocks, click **Undo** then use the **Brush** tool to fill in any gaps in your shapes.

6. In the **Sprites Pane**, click **Upload sprite from file**.

Find your **jollycoder** sprite and click **OK**.

The sprite will appear in the Sprites Pane.

---

7. Let's add a sound effect to play if the *Jolly Coder* hits a rock.

In the center of the screen, choose the **Sounds** tab.

New sound:

Click the **Choose sound from library** button.

Scroll down to choose **Tom drum**. Click **OK**.

---

8. Click the **Scripts** tab. Add this code to the **Jolly Coder** to make it sail until it hits a black rock. The **"Touching color"** block is in the **Sensing** group. Drop it in the hole in the **"Repeat until"** block.

Scripts

How to set the color for a "Touching" block

Click the color square.

touching color ☐ ?

The pointer changes.

On the Stage, click the color you want to check for.

The color is now set.

touching color ■ ?

```
when ⚑ clicked
set size to 20 %
go to x: -220 y: 0
repeat until < touching color ■ ? >
    point towards mouse-pointer▾
    move 1 steps
    ↰
play sound tom drum▾
```

Run the code below when the Green flag button is clicked:

Shrink the *Jolly Coder* to 20% of its size.

Move it to the left side of the Stage.

Repeat the code in the loop until the *Jolly Coder* hits a black rock:

Point the *Jolly Coder* toward the mouse.

Move the ship forward 1 step.

If the *Jolly Coder* hits a rock, play a sound effect. (Select Tom drum using the drop-down menu.)

---

9. Click the **Green flag** button to test your code.

Sail between those treacherous rocks until you reach Haunted Island.

To save your game, click the **File** menu then **Download to your computer**.

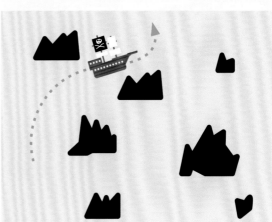

Finally you arrive at Haunted Island...

The ghost pirates must have hidden a treasure map around here. Let's find it! But don't get bitten by one of these poisonous crabs.

Find the ghost pirates' treasure map— but keep away from the scary crab!

CRAB COVE

1. Start a new file.

New

2. **Delete** the **cat** sprite.

3. Now we will draw Crab Cove!

Click **Backdrops**.

Choose the **Fill** tool.

Choose **pale yellow**.

Fill in the background.

4.

Choose the **Brush** tool.

Choose **green**.

Use the **Brush** to draw some small clumps of grass on the island.

5. Click **Choose sprite from library**.

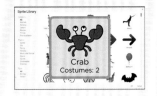

Scroll down then click the **Crab** icon.

 Click **OK**.

6. Now upload your pirate sprite.

Click **Upload sprite from file**.

Find your **pirate** sprite and click **OK**.

7. Click the **Scripts** tab and drag this code into the **Scripts Area** to control what happens to the pirate. The **"Touching"** block is in the **Sensing** group. Drop it in the hole in the **"Wait until"** block.

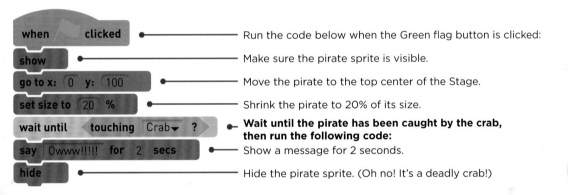

when clicked —————— Run the code below when the Green flag button is clicked:

show ———— Make sure the pirate sprite is visible.

go to x: 0 y: 100 ———— Move the pirate to the top center of the Stage.

set size to 20 % ———— Shrink the pirate to 20% of its size.

wait until touching Crab ? ← **Wait until the pirate has been caught by the crab, then run the following code:**

say Owww!!!!! for 2 secs ———— Show a message for 2 seconds.

hide ———— Hide the pirate sprite. (Oh no! It's a deadly crab!)

8. Drag in these 4 separate sets of code. They will make the pirate move when you press different keys on the keyboard.

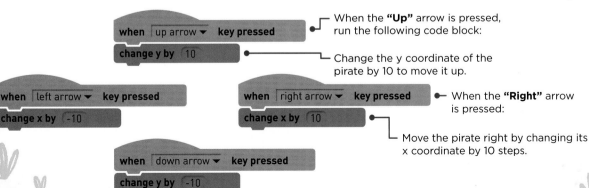

when up arrow key pressed ⌐ When the **"Up"** arrow is pressed, run the following code block:

change y by 10 ● ⌐ Change the y coordinate of the pirate by 10 to move it up.

when left arrow key pressed

change x by -10

when right arrow key pressed ● When the **"Right"** arrow is pressed:

change x by 10 ⌐ Move the pirate right by changing its x coordinate by 10 steps.

when down arrow key pressed

change y by -10

9. Now we will control how the crab will move around. Click the **Crab** in the **Sprites Pane**.

10. Click the **Scripts** tab. Build the code below to make the crab chase the pirate around the island.

Scripts

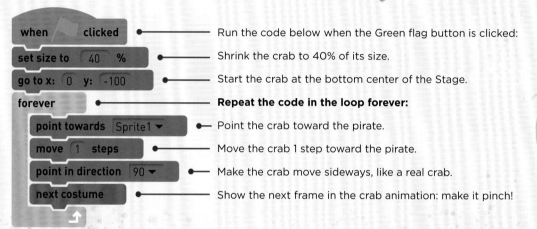

when clicked	Run the code below when the Green flag button is clicked:
set size to 40 %	Shrink the crab to 40% of its size.
go to x: 0 y: -100	Start the crab at the bottom center of the Stage.
forever	**Repeat the code in the loop forever:**
point towards Sprite1	Point the crab toward the pirate.
move 1 steps	Move the crab 1 step toward the pirate.
point in direction 90	Make the crab move sideways, like a real crab.
next costume	Show the next frame in the crab animation: make it pinch!

How the crab animation works

The animation works in a similar way to a cartoon on the TV or in a movie. By switching quickly between different images, we make it look as if the sprite is moving.

The crab sprite has two "costumes." Each costume is slightly different: one has the claws closed, one has them open. Changing the costumes quickly makes it look as if the crab is pinching!

Costume 1   **Costume 2**

11. Now we will draw the treasure map. Click the **Paint new sprite** button.

Choose the **Rectangle** tool.

At the bottom of the screen, click the **Solid rectangle**.

Select **blue** for the sea on the map.

44

12. Draw a large rectangle.

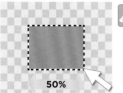

50%

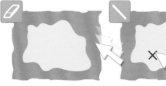

It should be about **half the width** of the Drawing Area. Make sure you get the size right. If not, click **Undo**.

Use the **Brush** to draw the island in yellow.

Fill it with color. (If the color leaks out, click **Undo**. Use the **Brush** to close up any gaps.)

Use the **Eraser** to make the edges of the map look old and worn.

Use the **Line** tool to add an X to mark the treasure, and any other details you like.

13. Click the **Scripts** tab. Drag over the code below to control the **map**.

Scripts

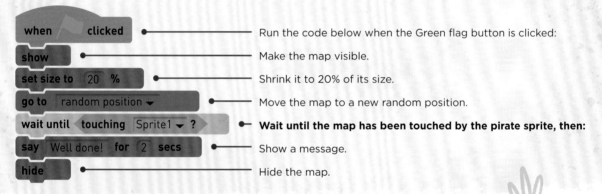

Run the code below when the Green flag button is clicked:

Make the map visible.

Shrink it to 20% of its size.

Move the map to a new random position.

Wait until the map has been touched by the pirate sprite, then:

Show a message.

Hide the map.

14. Click the **Green flag** to run your code. Use the arrow keys on the keyboard to move your pirate to the map—but watch out for the crab!

Don't forget to save your game by clicking **File** then **Download to your computer**.

You follow the map to the spot marked X.
You can only see sand, sand, and more sand...

Let's get digging, shipmate! Last one to find a jewel must walk the plank.

Walk the plank!

DIG FOR JEWELS

1. duplicate / delete — Start a new file and **delete** the **cat** sprite.

2. Backdrops

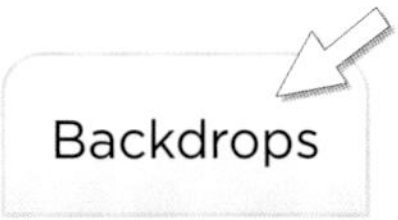

Click **Backdrops**.

Choose the **Fill** tool.

Choose **yellow**.

Fill in the background.

3. Upload your **pirate sprite**.

Sprite1

4. Click the **Scripts** tab. Drag over this code.

Scripts

when [green flag] clicked
set size to (20) %

Run the code below when the Green flag button is clicked:

Shrink the pirate to 20% of its size.

5. Now drag over the 4 separate sets of code below. They will make the pirate sprite move around the island when you press the arrow keys on your keyboard. Don't worry if you haven't learned about coordinates yet. Experimenting with these code blocks will help you come to grips with them.

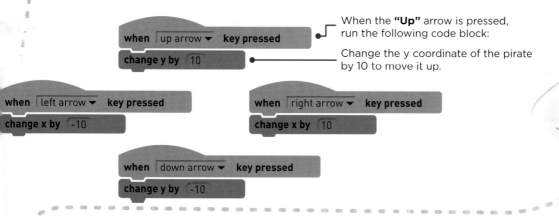

When the **"Up"** arrow is pressed, run the following code block:

Change the y coordinate of the pirate by 10 to move it up.

6. Click the **Green flag** button to test your code so far. Use the arrow keys to move your pirate around the Stage.

7.

Click the **Paint new sprite** button.

Select the **Brush** tool.

Choose **orange**.

Make a small orange mark just to the right of center.

8. To create our spray of sand, click the **Scripts** tab and drag this code over to the **Scripts Area** for your **sand** sprite. The **"Pick random"** block is in the **Operators** group. Drop it in the hole in the **"Point in direction"** block.

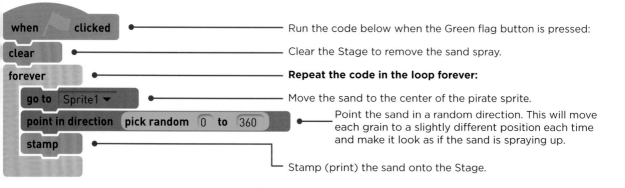

Run the code below when the Green flag button is pressed:

Clear the Stage to remove the sand spray.

Repeat the code in the loop forever:

Move the sand to the center of the pirate sprite.

Point the sand in a random direction. This will move each grain to a slightly different position each time and make it look as if the sand is spraying up.

Stamp (print) the sand onto the Stage.

9. Test your code to see the spray of sand as the pirate sprite moves around the Stage.

10. Now we will create our jewels.

Click **Choose sprite from library**.

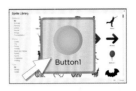

Click the **Button1** icon.

Click **OK**.

11. We need to hide the jewels when they are "buried" by making them the same color as the sand.

To do this, we will create a second costume for our jewel sprite, then color it the same shade of yellow as the background. Later, we will use our code to switch between these costumes when a jewel is found!

Click the **Costumes** tab.

Right click the **button1** icon in the **center** of the screen. On a Mac, hold **"Ctrl"** and **click**.

Click **Duplicate**.

12.

On the right side of the screen, choose the **Color a shape** tool.

Select the same **yellow** you used for the sand.

Click the edge of the button to color it.

And click it again in the center.

The sprite should now look like this.

13. Let's create a sound effect to play when a jewel is found.

Click on the **Sounds** tab.

Click the **Choose sound from library** button.

Scroll down to choose the **Fairydust** sound.

Click **OK**.

14. Click the **Scripts** tab and drag over this code for our **jewel** sprite.

Scripts

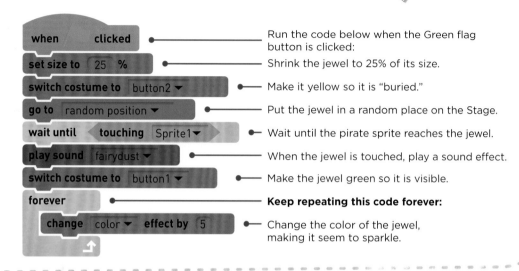

Run the code below when the Green flag button is clicked:

Shrink the jewel to 25% of its size.

Make it yellow so it is "buried."

Put the jewel in a random place on the Stage.

Wait until the pirate sprite reaches the jewel.

When the jewel is touched, play a sound effect.

Make the jewel green so it is visible.

Keep repeating this code forever:

Change the color of the jewel, making it seem to sparkle.

15. Test your code. The jewel will be hidden at first. Move your pirate around the screen to look for it. When you dig near it, the jewel will appear and sparkle.

16. **Right click** the **button1** icon in the **Sprites Pane**. On a Mac, hold **"Ctrl"** and **click**.

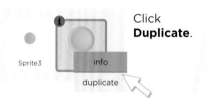

Click **Duplicate**.

17. Repeat step 16 to duplicate 3 more jewels.

18. Click the **Green flag** to dig up all Pirate Pierre's treasure.

Don't forget to click **File** then **Download to your computer** to save your game.

49

Just as you are celebrating your success, you are attacked...by the furious GHOST PIRATES!

We want that treasure!

Ooh-ar!

Take That!

Yikes!

GHOST SHIP

The ghost pirates grab the treasure and escape to their ship. Board the *Jolly Coder* and get the cannon ready to sink the ghost ship. Don't worry: the ghost pirates are already dead so you can't really hurt them!

1. duplicate delete — Start a new file and **delete** the **cat** sprite.

2. Backdrops — Click **Backdrops** to create a background for our battle.

3.

Choose the **Fill** tool.

Choose **light sea blue**.

Fill in the background.

Choose the **Rectangle** tool.

At the bottom of the screen, click the **Solid rectangle**.

Add some sky at the top, using a slightly **brighter blue**.

Use **brown** to add the deck of the *Jolly Coder* at the bottom.

4. To create a cannonball, click the **Choose sprite from library** button.

Sprite Library

Ball

Click the **Ball** icon.

OK

Click **OK**.

5. Click the **Scripts** tab and add these 2 separate sets of code for the **cannonball**.

Scripts

```
when   clicked
go to x: 0  y: -120
```
— Run the code below when the Green flag button is clicked:
— Move the cannonball to the bottom center of the Stage.

```
when  space ▼  key pressed
repeat until    touching edge ▼ ?
    change size by -1
    change y by 5

go to x: 0  y: -120
set size to 100 %
```
— When the **"Space"** key is pressed, run this code:
— Repeat the code in the loop until the cannonball hits the edge of the Stage:
— Make the cannonball smaller so it looks like it is getting farther away.
— Move the cannonball up the screen.
— Once the cannonball reaches the screen edge, run this code:
— Move the cannonball back to the bottom center of the Stage.
— Make the cannonball normal size again.

6. Test your code so far. Try pressing the **"Space"** bar to fire the cannonball.

7. To make the ghost ship, we will use our old *Jolly Coder* sprite.

In the **Sprites Pane**, click **Upload sprite from file**.

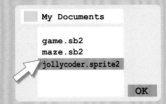

My Documents

game.sb2
maze.sb2
jollycoder.sprite2

OK

Find your **jollycoder** sprite and click **OK**.

Sprite1

The sprite will appear in the Sprites Pane.

8. Now we will make some changes to the *Jolly Coder* as it doesn't look very ghostly. Click the **Costumes** tab.

Costumes

Select the **Fill** tool and choose **black**. Click inside all the parts of the *Jolly Coder*.

Use the **Eraser** to make the sails look tattered and ghostly.

9. We need the ghost ship to sail back and forth across the Stage in a straight line. To make it move in this way, we need to stop it from rotating.

Sprites

Sprite1

Find the ghost ship in the **Sprites Pane**.

Click the **i** in the blue circle.

Sprite1

x: -51   y:71   **direction:** 90

rotation style ●

Click the **arrow**.

Click the **white triangle**.

10. Let's add a sound effect to play when the ghost ship is hit by the cannonball.

Sounds

Click on the **Sounds** tab.

New sound:

Click the **Choose sound from library** button.

lo geh tabla

Scroll down and choose the **Lo geh tabla** sound.

OK

Click **OK**.

11. Click the **Scripts** tab and move this code to the **Scripts Area** to control the **Ghost Ship**. Remember that the **"Pick random"** block is in the **Operators** group—drop it in the hole in the **"Change effect"** block.

Scripts

when ◄ clicked	Run the code when the Green flag button is clicked:
set size to 20 %	Shrink the ghost ship to 20% of its size.
go to x: -150 y: 125	Start the ghost ship at the top left of the Stage.
repeat until ◄ touching color ?	**Repeat the code in the loop until the ship sinks to the bottom of the screen (to set the color to brown, see page 41):**
move 3 steps	Move the ghost ship forward 3 steps.
change ghost▼ effect by pick random -10 to 10	Use a special effect to make the ghost ship shimmer and appear transparent.
if touching Ball▼ ? then	**If the ghost ship is hit by the cannonball:**
play sound lo geh tabla ▼	Play a sound effect.
change color▼ effect by 25	Make the ghost ship light up as if exploding.
change y by -5	Make the ghost ship sink a little.
if on edge, bounce	If the ghost ship reaches the side of the Stage, change direction.
say You have sunk the Ghost Ship!	**If the ghost ship sinks to the bottom, run this code:** Show a message celebrating that the ship has sunk!

The sinking ghost ship explodes, filling the sky with dust and...Pirate Pierre's treasure!

53

CATCH THE TREASURE

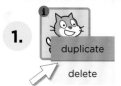

1. Start a new file and **delete** the **cat** sprite.

2. Click the **Stage** icon.

Click **Choose backdrop from library**.

Choose **Beach rio** then click **OK**.

3. Upload your **pirate** sprite.

4. Click the **Scripts** tab and drag this code over to the **Scripts Area** to control how the **pirate sprite** moves.

Scripts

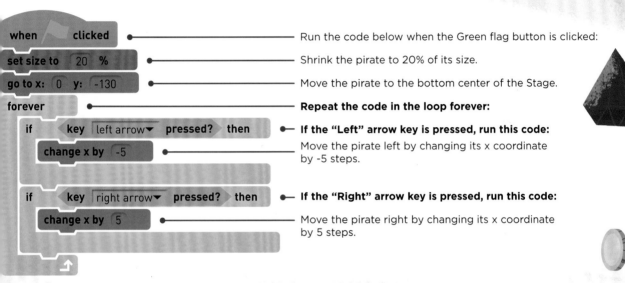

when 🏴 clicked ———— Run the code below when the Green flag button is clicked:

set size to 20 % ———— Shrink the pirate to 20% of its size.

go to x: 0 y: -130 ———— Move the pirate to the bottom center of the Stage.

forever ———— **Repeat the code in the loop forever:**

if key left arrow▾ pressed? then ●— **If the "Left" arrow key is pressed, run this code:**

change x by -5 ———— Move the pirate left by changing its x coordinate by -5 steps.

if key right arrow▾ pressed? then ●— **If the "Right" arrow key is pressed, run this code:**

change x by 5 ———— Move the pirate right by changing its x coordinate by 5 steps.

5. Click the **Choose sprite from library** button to add some treasure.

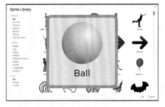
Ball

Scroll down then click the **Ball** icon.

We will use this as a gold coin.

OK Click **OK**.

6. Let's create a sound effect that will play every time a gold coin is caught.

Sounds

Click on the **Sounds** tab.

New sound:

Click the **Choose sound from library** button.

Scroll down and choose the **Hi tun tabla** sound.

OK

Click **OK**.

7. It will make our game more fun if we can count how many gold coins we have caught. To do this, we will use a special part of our program, called a variable. Variables are a way that computer programs store values that can change—such as the score. We will call our variable **coins**.

Sound
Pen
Data

Click the **Scripts** tab then the **Data** group.

Make a Variable

Click **Make a variable**.

Variable name: coins

Call it **coins**.

OK

Then click **OK**.

8. Now drag this code into the **Scripts Area** to control how the **gold coin** moves and gets caught. The orange blocks are in the **Data** group. These blocks control our score.

Scripts

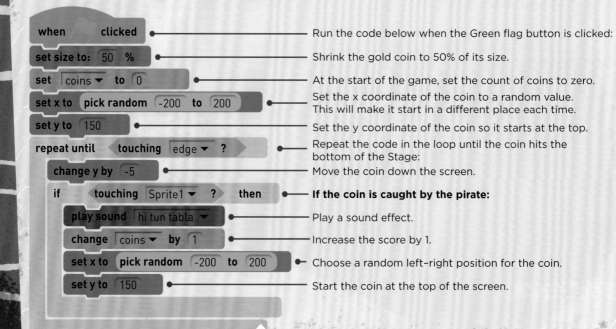

when clicked — Run the code below when the Green flag button is clicked:

set size to: 50 % — Shrink the gold coin to 50% of its size.

set coins to 0 — At the start of the game, set the count of coins to zero.

set x to pick random -200 to 200 — Set the x coordinate of the coin to a random value. This will make it start in a different place each time.

set y to 150 — Set the y coordinate of the coin so it starts at the top.

repeat until touching edge ? — Repeat the code in the loop until the coin hits the bottom of the Stage:

change y by -5 — Move the coin down the screen.

if touching Sprite1 ? then — **If the coin is caught by the pirate:**

play sound hi tun tabla — Play a sound effect.

change coins by 1 — Increase the score by 1.

set x to pick random -200 to 200 — Choose a random left–right position for the coin.

set y to 150 — Start the coin at the top of the screen.

9. Click the **Green flag** then use the arrow keys to move left and right, catching as much treasure as you can! Your game should look like this:

Don't forget to click **File** then **Download to your computer** to save your game.

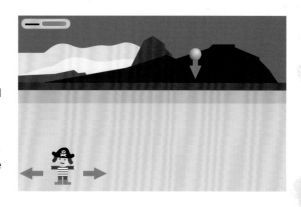

Thankee kindly, shipmate. Shiver me timbers, without your help my treasure would have been lost beneath the foaming waves. YO HO HO!

Shiver me timbers!

CODE YOUR OWN JUNGLE ADVENTURE

You get a call from Captain Maria, the brave explorer. She asks you to meet her at the Museum of Ancient Treasures...

Welcome, old friend. After many years of searching, I have found an ancient map revealing the location of the Lost City of Gold, deep in the rainforest. I must travel there quickly to save its priceless treasures from robbers. But I cannot do it alone! Will you help me?

You agree to help Captain Maria on her dangerous journey! Before you set off, you must dress yourself in suitable clothing for an expedition.

1. Open **Scratch**.

Let's delete the cat sprite. In the **Sprites Pane, right click** the **cat**. On a Mac, hold the **"Ctrl"** key then **click.**

Choose **Delete**.

2. To start drawing yourself as an explorer, click the **Paint new sprite** button in the **Sprites Pane**.

3. Now you should be able to see the **Drawing Area**.

 Choose the **Ellipse tool.**

 At the bottom of the screen, click the **Solid ellipse**.

4. Select a **skin color**.

Draw your head by dragging the mouse.

5.  Choose the **Rectangle** tool and draw 2 rectangles for your arms and body.

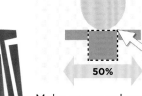

50%

Make your explorer **half the width** of the Drawing Area.

6. Use rectangles to make your pants and boots.

 If things go wrong, click **Undo** and go back a step.

7. Choose the **Line tool.**

Set it to a **medium thickness**.

8. Draw a belt, then add 2 lines for the brim of your hat.

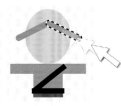

9. Choose the **Fill** tool then click the top of your head.

10. Use the **Brush** tool to add final details.

Now turn the page to find out how to save your explorer drawing so you can use it on your expedition. Quick—turn over!

Oops. I packed a basket of supplies for the trip, but I can't remember where I left it! Can you find it? I think it's somewhere in the museum...

FIND THE FOOD

1. Before you do anything else, save your explorer sprite so you can use it for all the other activities in this adventure.

In the **Sprites Pane, right click** on the **explorer** sprite icon. On a Mac computer, hold the **"Ctrl"** key and **click**.

delete

save to local file

Click **Save to local file**.

Type in **explorer** as a name for your sprite and click **OK**.

2. In the center of the screen, click the **Scripts** tab so Scratch is ready for you to add some code to make your explorer move.

Scripts   Costumes

3. Drag these blocks into the **Scripts Area**, in this order. Remember that the color of each block tells us which group it is in. So the **"When green flag clicked"** block is in the **Events** group. The blue blocks are in the **Motion** group. All the purple blocks are in the **Looks** group. The **"Repeat"** loop block is in **Control**. You can click in the white box in a block in order to change the message or number, so click in the **"Think"** and **"Say"** blocks to type in the words.

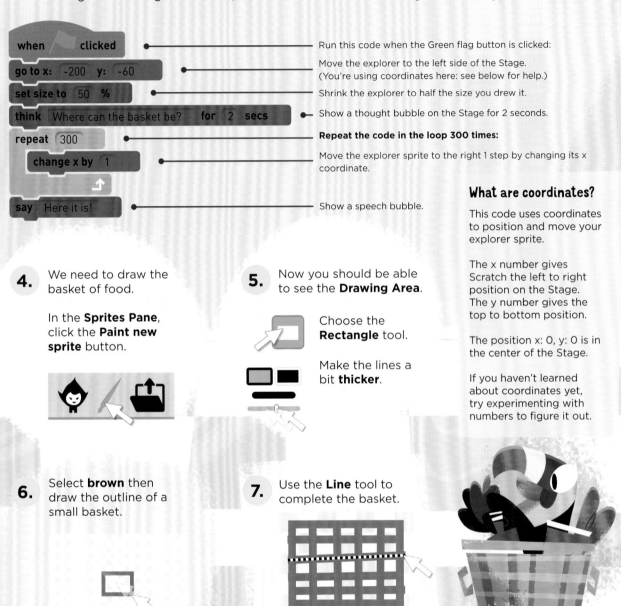

when ⚑ clicked — Run this code when the Green flag button is clicked:

go to x: -200 y: -60 — Move the explorer to the left side of the Stage. (You're using coordinates here: see below for help.)

set size to 50 % — Shrink the explorer to half the size you drew it.

think Where can the basket be? for 2 secs — Show a thought bubble on the Stage for 2 seconds.

repeat 300 — **Repeat the code in the loop 300 times:**

change x by 1 — Move the explorer sprite to the right 1 step by changing its x coordinate.

say Here it is! — Show a speech bubble.

What are coordinates?

This code uses coordinates to position and move your explorer sprite.

The x number gives Scratch the left to right position on the Stage. The y number gives the top to bottom position.

The position x: 0, y: 0 is in the center of the Stage.

If you haven't learned about coordinates yet, try experimenting with numbers to figure it out.

4. We need to draw the basket of food.

In the **Sprites Pane**, click the **Paint new sprite** button.

5. Now you should be able to see the **Drawing Area**.

Choose the **Rectangle** tool.

Make the lines a bit **thicker**.

6. Select **brown** then draw the outline of a small basket.

7. Use the **Line** tool to complete the basket.

8. Drag the basket to the **right side** of the Stage. Then click the **Green flag** button at the top right of the **Stage**. Your explorer should find Captain Maria's lost basket!

To save your code, click the **File** menu, then **Download to your computer**. Then to use it again, you can click **File** and **Upload from your computer**.

Captain Maria takes you into the museum gardens, where her hot-air balloon is waiting...

DISASTER! My hot-air balloon has been punctured. We can't take off for the rainforest until it is fixed!

Fix Captain Maria's balloon by drawing your own hot-air balloon sprite.

HOT-AIR BALLOON

90%

Your drawing should be **almost as tall** as the Drawing Area. If not, your games might not work. If things go wrong, click **Undo**.

1. Start a new Scratch file.

Delete the cat sprite. In the **Sprites Pane**, **right click** the cat. On a Mac, hold the **"Ctrl"** key then **click.**

Click **Delete**.

2. Start drawing your balloon by clicking the **Paint new sprite** button in the **Sprites Pane**.

You should now see the **Drawing Area**.

3.  Choose the **Ellipse** tool.

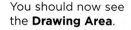 At the bottom of the screen, click the **Solid ellipse**.

4.  Select **red**.

Draw a large oval in the top center of the Drawing Area.

5.  Choose the **Rectangle** tool.

Add a small rectangle.

6. Select **brown** and draw the basket.

7. Choose the **Line** tool.

 Make the line **thicker**. Add some detail.

8. Draw two **yellow** lines across the balloon.

9. Draw **brown** lines to join the balloon to the basket.

10. Use the **Zoom** control so you can add small details more easily. Zoom in for the next step.

200%

Zoom out   Zoom in

11.  Use the **Brush** tool to draw yourself and Maria.

12.

Decorate the balloon!

13. Now save your balloon sprite so you can use it to take off...

In the Sprites Pane, **right click** your **balloon**. On a Mac, hold **"Ctrl"** and **click**.

delete
save to local file

Click **Save to local file**.

Type in **balloon** as a name for your sprite and click **OK**.

Thank you for fixing my balloon! Climb aboard and we can go...

UP, UP, AND AWAY!

1. Start a new Scratch file.

File ▾

New

Right click the **cat**. On a Mac, hold **"Ctrl"** and **click**.

duplicate

delete

Click **Delete**.

---

2. You need to upload the hot-air balloon sprite you drew on the previous page. If you haven't already drawn it, turn back to page 62 and follow steps 2 to 13.

In the **Sprites Pane**, click **Upload sprite from file**.

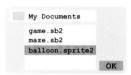

My Documents

game.sb2
maze.sb2
balloon.sprite2

OK

Find your file and click **OK**.

Sprite1

The sprite will appear in the Sprites Pane.

---

3. Click the **Scripts** tab and drag this code into the **Scripts Area** to make your balloon fly.

Scripts

when [green flag] clicked — Run the code below when the Green flag button is clicked:

go to x: 0 y: -85 — Start the balloon at the center bottom of the Stage.

set size to 40 % — Shrink the balloon to 40% of the size you drew it.

forever — **Repeat the code in the loop forever:**

point towards mouse-pointer ▾ — Make the balloon point toward the mouse pointer.

move 1 steps — Move the balloon forward 1 step.

point in direction 90 ▾ — Keep the balloon upright by making it point to the right.

64

4. Now we will draw a background for our balloon
to take off in front of.

In the **Sprites Pane**, click the **Stage** icon.

Click the **Backdrops** tab.

Select the **Fill** tool.

Choose **light blue**.

Fill in the background by clicking in the **Drawing Area**.

5. Now let's draw some grass on the ground.

   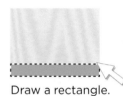

Select the **Rectangle** tool.

At the bottom of the screen, click the **Solid rectangle**.

Choose **dark green**.

Draw a rectangle.

6. Now click the **Green flag** button to test your code. Move your mouse pointer around and the balloon will fly slowly toward it. It's time to take off for the rainforest!

Remember to save your game by clicking the **File** menu then **Download to your computer**.

As you fly through the Mysterious Mountains, your skills are put to the test yet again...

We are going to crash into the mountain! Steer us into that cave and—hopefully—out the other side.

CAVE CRASH

1. Start a new file.

File ▼

New

Delete the **cat** sprite.

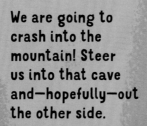

duplicate

delete

2. Now we will draw our cave.

Stage
1 Backdrop

Click the **Stage** button in the **Sprites Pane**.

Backdrops

Click the **Backdrops** tab.

Select the **Fill** tool.

Choose **dark brown**.

Click in the **Drawing Area** to fill it.

3.

Choose the **Line** tool.

Choose **dark gray**.

Make the line width **thicker**.

Draw the bottom of the cave.

4. Use lines to draw the top of the cave.

Leave a gap between the top and bottom!

5. Color in the cave with the **Fill** tool.

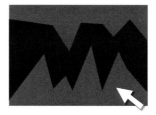

If the color leaks out, click **Undo** and draw a line over any gaps.

6. To upload your balloon sprite, click **Upload sprite from file**.

My Documents
game.sb2
maze.sb2
balloon.sprite2
OK

Find your file and click **OK**.

The sprite will appear.

Sprite1

7. Click **Scripts** then add this code to make the balloon fly until it hits the rocks in the cave. You will find the **"Touching color"** block in the **Sensing** group. Drop it in the hole in the **"Repeat until"** loop.

 Scripts

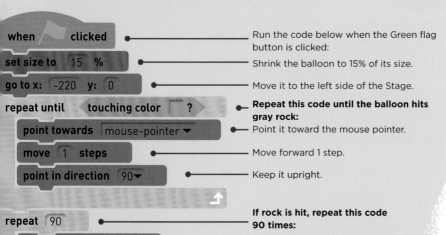

when ⚑ clicked — Run the code below when the Green flag button is clicked:

set size to 15 % — Shrink the balloon to 15% of its size.

go to x: -220 y: 0 — Move it to the left side of the Stage.

repeat until touching color ? — **Repeat this code until the balloon hits gray rock:**

point towards mouse-pointer ▼ — Point it toward the mouse pointer.

move 1 steps — Move forward 1 step.

point in direction 90▼ — Keep it upright.

repeat 90 — **If rock is hit, repeat this code 90 times:**

turn ↻ 8 degrees — Rotate the balloon 8 degrees.

change y by -4 — Move it down.

How to set the color for a 'Touching' block

Click the color square.

touching color ?

The pointer changes.

On the Stage, click the color you want to check for.

The color is now set.

touching color ?

8. Click the **Green flag** button to fly safely through the cave!

At last you are soaring above the rainforest. But so are thousands of bloodthirsty bats!

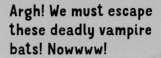

Argh! We must escape these deadly vampire bats! Nowwww!

BAT ATTACK

1. Start a new file and **delete** the **cat** sprite.

duplicate

delete

2. Now we will draw a sky background for our balloon to fly through.

Stage
1 Backdrop

In the **Sprites Pane**, click the **Stage** icon.

Backdrops

Click the **Backdrops** tab.

Select the **Fill** tool.

Click **blue**.

Fill in the background.

3.

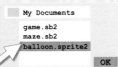

My Documents
game.sb2
maze.sb2
balloon.sprite2

OK

Find your file and click **OK**.

Sprite1

The sprite will appear.

To upload your balloon sprite, click **Upload sprite from file**.

4. Drag this code into the **Scripts Area** to make the **hot-air balloon** fly.

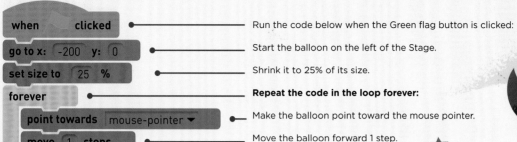

Code	Explanation
when [flag] clicked	Run the code below when the Green flag button is clicked:
go to x: -200 y: 0	Start the balloon on the left of the Stage.
set size to 25 %	Shrink it to 25% of its size.
forever	**Repeat the code in the loop forever:**
point towards mouse-pointer ▼	Make the balloon point toward the mouse pointer.
move 1 steps	Move the balloon forward 1 step.
point in direction 90 ▼	Keep the balloon upright.

5. To create a bat, click the **Choose sprite from library** button in the **Sprites Pane**.

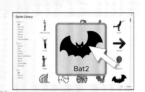

Scroll down then click the **Bat2** icon.

OK

Click **OK**.

6. Drag this code into the **Scripts Area** to make the **bat** flap its wings until it touches the hot-air balloon.

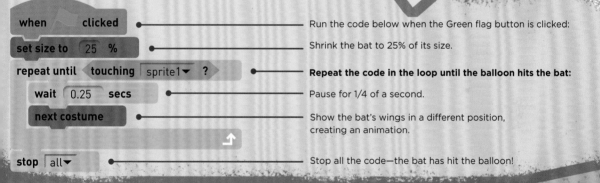

Code	Explanation
when [flag] clicked	Run the code below when the Green flag button is clicked:
set size to 25 %	Shrink the bat to 25% of its size.
repeat until touching sprite1 ▼ ?	**Repeat the code in the loop until the balloon hits the bat:**
wait 0.25 secs	Pause for 1/4 of a second.
next costume	Show the bat's wings in a different position, creating an animation.
stop all ▼	Stop all the code—the bat has hit the balloon!

How the bat animation works

The animation works in a similar way to a cartoon on the TV or in a movie. By switching quickly between different images, we make it look as if the sprite is moving.

The bat sprite has two "costumes." Each costume is slightly different: one has the wings up, one has them down. Changing the costumes quickly makes it look as if the bat is flying!

Costume 1

Costume 2

7. **Right click** (**"Ctrl" click** on a Mac) the bat and choose **Duplicate**.

info
duplicate

8. Drag the new bat into a space.

9. Repeat step 7 to add more bats.

Now click the **Green flag**!

You touch down in the rainforest, hopefully not too far from the fabled City of Gold. Captain Maria wades into a murky-looking river...

YIKES! THE WATER IS INFESTED WITH DEADLY ANACONDAS!

You must cross the river to reach the City of Gold, so you have no choice but to wade in after Captain Maria. Make sure you avoid the anacondas.

CROSS THE RIVER

1. Start a new file. **Delete** the cat sprite.

duplicate
delete

2.  Backdrops

Click **Backdrops**.

Select the **Fill** tool.

Click **dark green**.

Fill in the background.

3. Now we need to draw the river.

Select the **Brush** tool.

Click **blue**.

Make the brush width **thicker**.

Draw one side of the river.

Next draw the other side.

Fill in the river.

Choose **green** and use the **Brush** to draw small islands.

4. Let's draw a deadly anaconda.

Click the **Paint new sprite** button.

The anaconda must be about **three-quarters of the width** of the Drawing Area.

75%

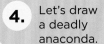
Choose **red** and select the **Brush** tool.

Make the brush **very thick**.

Draw the snake's body.

Add a head.

Make the brush **thinner** to draw eyes and a tongue.

5. Click the **Scripts** tab and drag this code into the **Scripts Area** to make the **anaconda** swim.

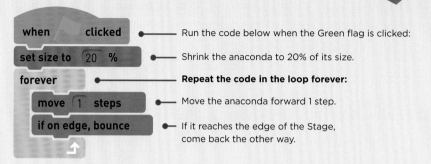

when ▢ clicked	Run the code below when the Green flag is clicked:
set size to 20 %	Shrink the anaconda to 20% of its size.
forever	**Repeat the code in the loop forever:**
move 1 steps	Move the anaconda forward 1 step.
if on edge, bounce	If it reaches the edge of the Stage, come back the other way.

Click the **Green flag** to test your code. You may need to drag the snake into the river. It should then swim slowly from side to side.

6. When the anaconda swims back, it will be upside down. To fix this, do the following:

In the **Sprites Pane**, click the blue **i**.

Set the **rotation style** of the anaconda to the center option, **left-right**.

Click the **blue triangle** button when you have finished.

7. Make some more anacondas. **Right click (or "Ctrl" click)** the anaconda and choose **Duplicate**.

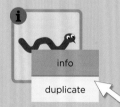

8. **Drag** the new anaconda into a space.

Repeat step 7 until you have around **6** snakes.

9. Upload your **explorer** sprite by clicking **Upload sprite from file**.

Find your file and click **OK**.

The sprite will appear.

10. Click the **Scripts** tab and drag this code into the **Scripts Area** for the **explorer** sprite.

```
when [flag] clicked
show
set size to 20 %
go to x: 0 y: 160
wait until < touching color [ ] ? >
say [Aggghhh!] for 2 secs
hide
```

Run the code below when the Green flag button is clicked:

Make sure the explorer sprite is visible.

Shrink the explorer to 20% of its size.

Start the explorer at the top center of the Stage.

Wait until the explorer is touching a snake (for help with this block, turn to page 67, step 7):

Then show a message for 2 seconds.

Make the explorer disappear. (Whoops, you've been eaten!)

11. Now add these 4 separate groups of code (called "scripts") for the **explorer**. Each of the scripts runs when a different arrow key is pressed on the keyboard. Each script changes either the x coordinate (how far across the Stage the sprite is) or the y coordinate (how far up it is).

```
when [up arrow ▼] key pressed
change y by 5
```

When the **"Up"** arrow key is pressed:

Move the explorer up 5 steps.

```
when [left arrow ▼] key pressed
change x by -5
```

```
when [right arrow ▼] key pressed
change x by 5
```

```
when [down arrow ▼] key pressed
change y by -5
```

12. Use the **arrow** keys to move your explorer across the river. Avoid the anacondas!

You trudge through the rainforest until, between the trees, you glimpse it... the **City of Gold**!

I can hardly believe my eyes! After all these years of searching...priceless treasures are hidden inside that golden pyramid. Let's go inside! The only problem is that monkey guarding the entrance. He looks a little bit annoyed...

MONKEY MADNESS

Can you climb to the top of the pyramid, avoiding the bananas thrown by the furious monkey?

1. Start a new file and **delete** the **cat** sprite.

2. Let's start to draw a background for our game.

Click **Backdrops**.	Select the **Fill** tool.	Click **light blue**.	Choose **Gradient fill**.	Fill the background by clicking in the Drawing Area.

3. Draw some grass on the ground.

Select the **Rectangle** tool.	Click the **Solid rectangle**.	Choose **dark green**.	Draw a rectangle.

4. Now draw the golden pyramid.

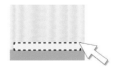

Select the **Rectangle** tool.	Choose **yellow**.	Carefully draw the first level.	If it is not in exactly the right place, use the handles to move it.

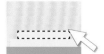

Draw **4** more rectangles to add each level of the pyramid. If a rectangle is not in the correct place, adjust it with the handles or click **Undo**.

5. Draw the path that leads to the top of the pyramid.

Select the **Rectangle** tool.

Choose the **golden** color below the yellow.

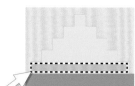

Carefully draw a path on the pyramid.

If a rectangle is not in exactly the right place, use the handles to move it or use the **Undo** button and try again.

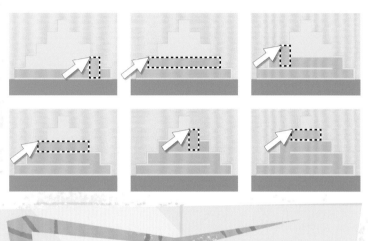

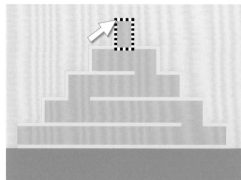

Add rectangles in the pattern shown here to complete the path to the top. In the end, your temple should look like this!

6. To create the monkey, click the **Choose sprite from library** button.

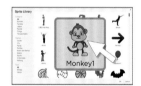

Scroll down then click the **Monkey1** icon.

Click **OK**.

7. Click the **Shrink** button in the Scratch **Menu bar**, then click the monkey on the **Stage** several times to make it much smaller.

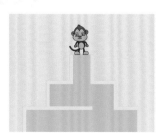

Drag the monkey to the **top** of the pyramid.

8. To give the monkey his bananas, click the **Choose sprite from library** button.

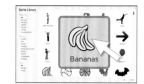

Scroll down then click the **Bananas** icon.

Click **OK**.

9. Click **Scripts** then add this code for the **bananas** sprite. The code will make the bananas look as if they are being thrown by the monkey.

Scripts

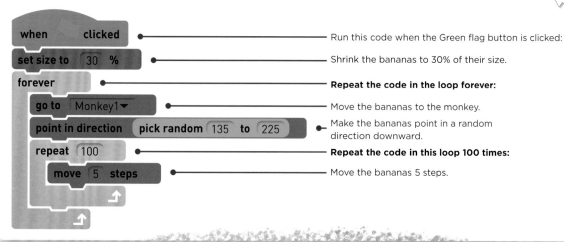

when clicked	Run this code when the Green flag button is clicked:
set size to 30 %	Shrink the bananas to 30% of their size.
forever	**Repeat the code in the loop forever:**
go to Monkey1 ▼	Move the bananas to the monkey.
point in direction pick random 135 to 225	Make the bananas point in a random direction downward.
repeat 100	**Repeat the code in this loop 100 times:**
move 5 steps	Move the bananas 5 steps.

Setting a random direction

point in direction | pick random 1 to 10

The **"Pick random"** block is in the **Operators** group. It commands Scratch to pick a random number between the two numbers you type into its holes.

Drag the block from its left-hand side. As you drag it over the white circle on the **"Point in direction"** block, the border will glow to show it is in the right place.

10. To upload your explorer sprite, click **Upload sprite from file**.

My Documents
game.sb2
maze.sb2
explorer.sprite2
OK

Find your file and click **OK**.

Sprite1

The sprite will appear.

11. Click **Scripts** then add this code to control the **explorer** sprite. (There are 3 different sprites in this game, so make sure you've got the right one selected in the **Sprites Pane**.)

Scripts

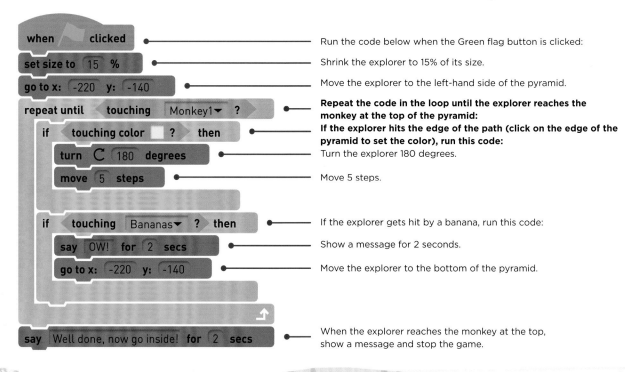

```
when [flag] clicked
set size to 15 %
go to x: -220 y: -140
repeat until < touching Monkey1 ? >
    if < touching color [ ] ? > then
        turn C 180 degrees
        move 5 steps
    if < touching Bananas ? > then
        say OW! for 2 secs
        go to x: -220 y: -140
say Well done, now go inside! for 2 secs
```

- Run the code below when the Green flag button is clicked:
- Shrink the explorer to 15% of its size.
- Move the explorer to the left-hand side of the pyramid.
- **Repeat the code in the loop until the explorer reaches the monkey at the top of the pyramid:**
- **If the explorer hits the edge of the path (click on the edge of the pyramid to set the color), run this code:**
- Turn the explorer 180 degrees.
- Move 5 steps.
- If the explorer gets hit by a banana, run this code:
- Show a message for 2 seconds.
- Move the explorer to the bottom of the pyramid.
- When the explorer reaches the monkey at the top, show a message and stop the game.

12. Now add these four separate scripts. They will make the explorer move up, down, left, or right when you use the arrow keys on your keyboard.

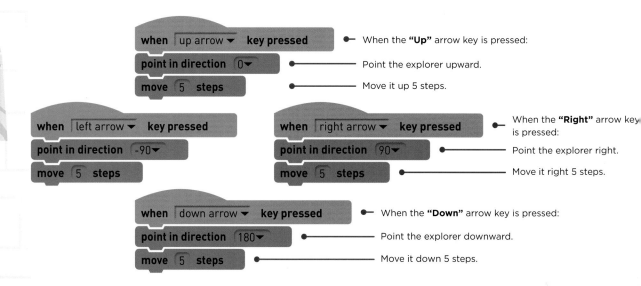

```
when up arrow key pressed
point in direction 0
move 5 steps
```

- When the **"Up"** arrow key is pressed:
- Point the explorer upward.
- Move it up 5 steps.

```
when left arrow key pressed
point in direction -90
move 5 steps
```

```
when right arrow key pressed
point in direction 90
move 5 steps
```

- When the **"Right"** arrow key is pressed:
- Point the explorer right.
- Move it right 5 steps.

```
when down arrow key pressed
point in direction 180
move 5 steps
```

- When the **"Down"** arrow key is pressed:
- Point the explorer downward.
- Move it down 5 steps.

13. We need to change the way the explorer moves so it does not rotate when it changes direction—we want it to stay upright!

In the **Sprites Pane**, click the blue **i** circle on the **explorer** icon.

Set the **rotation style** to the right-hand option, **no-rotate**.

Now click the **blue triangle** button.

14. Press the **Green flag** button to battle the angry monkey!

Don't forget to save your game by choosing **File** and **Download to your computer**.

Not fitting in?

If your paths are too thin, the explorer may not be able to fit through them.

If so, reduce the percentage in the **"Set size to"** block in step 11. Try **12%** or less.

HURRAY! LET'S GO INSIDE!

OOH OOH AAH AAH!

You enter the pyramid. It is dark and you are not alone...

OoooOoOOH

Help me collect the treasure, old friend. There is nothing to fear here!

MAZE OF GOLD

Collect the treasure, but avoid the ghostly ghoul!

1. Start a new file and **delete** the **cat** sprite.

duplicate

delete

2. Draw a pyramid on the backdrop, just like on page 75, steps 2–4.

3.

Select the **Rectangle** tool.

Choose **black**.

Carefully draw a corridor from the top of the pyramid.

Add more corridors to complete your maze. Make sure they are not too small for the explorer to fit through.

4. Now upload your **explorer** sprite.

Click **Upload sprite from file**. Find your file and click **OK**.

5. Add a ghost to haunt the corridors. Click **Choose sprite from library**.

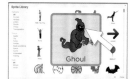

Click **Ghoul**.

Click **OK**.

6. Click **Scripts** then add this code to make the **ghoul** move around the pyramid.

Scripts

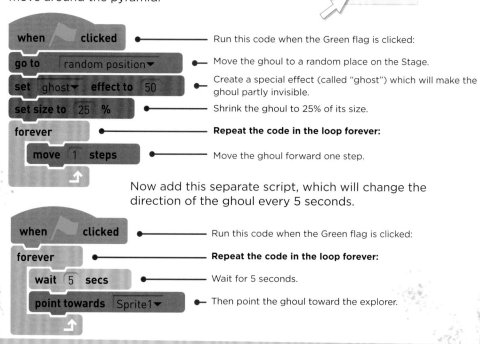

```
when [flag] clicked                    ── Run this code when the Green flag is clicked:
go to [random position▼]               ── Move the ghoul to a random place on the Stage.
set [ghost▼] effect to [50]            ── Create a special effect (called "ghost") which will make the
                                          ghoul partly invisible.
set size to [25] %                     ── Shrink the ghoul to 25% of its size.
forever                                ── **Repeat the code in the loop forever:**
    move [1] steps                     ── Move the ghoul forward one step.
```

Now add this separate script, which will change the direction of the ghoul every 5 seconds.

```
when [flag] clicked                    ── Run this code when the Green flag is clicked:
forever                                ── **Repeat the code in the loop forever:**
    wait [5] secs                      ── Wait for 5 seconds.
    point towards [Sprite1▼]           ── Then point the ghoul toward the explorer.
```

7. We will stop the **explorer** sprite from turning upside down when it changes direction.

Sprite1

In the **Sprites Pane**, click the blue **i**.

rotation style ↻ ⟷

Set the **rotation style** to the right-hand option, **no-rotate**.

Click the **blue triangle** button.

8. Let's count how many coins we find. We'll use a special part of our program, called a variable. Variables are a way that programs store values that can change—such as the score.

Sound
Pen
Data

Click the **Data** group.

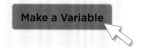

Click **Make a variable**.

Variable name: [score]

Call it **score**.

Click **OK**.

9. Click the **Scripts** tab and add this code for the **explorer** sprite. The orange blocks are in the **Data** group. The green **"Equals (=)"** block is in the **Operators** group. Drop the little **"Score"** block into it.

Scripts

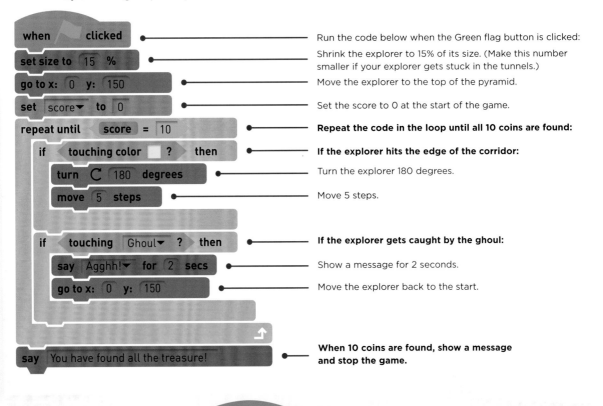

when [flag] clicked ———— Run the code below when the Green flag button is clicked:

set size to 15 % ———— Shrink the explorer to 15% of its size. (Make this number smaller if your explorer gets stuck in the tunnels.)

go to x: 0 y: 150 ———— Move the explorer to the top of the pyramid.

set score to 0 ———— Set the score to 0 at the start of the game.

repeat until score = 10 ———— **Repeat the code in the loop until all 10 coins are found:**

  if touching color ? then ———— **If the explorer hits the edge of the corridor:**

    turn ↻ 180 degrees ———— Turn the explorer 180 degrees.

    move 5 steps ———— Move 5 steps.

  if touching Ghoul ? then ———— **If the explorer gets caught by the ghoul:**

    say Agghh! for 2 secs ———— Show a message for 2 seconds.

    go to x: 0 y: 150 ———— Move the explorer back to the start.

say You have found all the treasure! ———— **When 10 coins are found, show a message and stop the game.**

10. Now add these 4 separate scripts to make the explorer move.

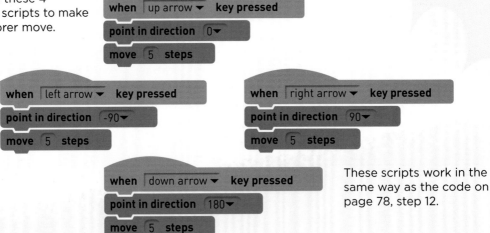

when [up arrow] key pressed
point in direction 0
move 5 steps

when [left arrow] key pressed
point in direction -90
move 5 steps

when [right arrow] key pressed
point in direction 90
move 5 steps

when [down arrow] key pressed
point in direction 180
move 5 steps

These scripts work in the same way as the code on page 78, step 12.

11. To create a gold coin, click the **Choose sprite from library** button.

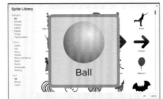

Ball

Click the **Ball** icon.

 OK

Click **OK**.

12. Click **Scripts** and add this code to make the **coin** disappear when the explorer finds it.

Scripts

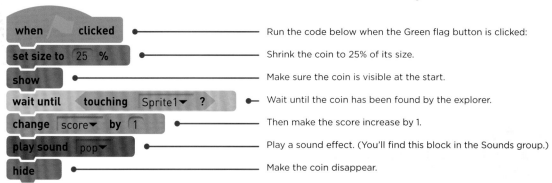

when 🏳 clicked	Run the code below when the Green flag button is clicked:
set size to 25 %	Shrink the coin to 25% of its size.
show	Make sure the coin is visible at the start.
wait until touching Sprite1 ▾ ?	Wait until the coin has been found by the explorer.
change score ▾ by 1	Then make the score increase by 1.
play sound pop ▾	Play a sound effect. (You'll find this block in the Sounds group.)
hide	Make the coin disappear.

13. In the **Sprites Pane, right click** (or **"Ctrl" click**) the **Ball** sprite. Choose **Duplicate**.

14. Drag the new coin into a gap in the corridors. You may find it easier to do this after pressing the **Green flag** to shrink the coins.

Repeat step 13 until you have 10 coins.

15. Click the **Green flag** to collect all the gold. Don't forget to save your game.

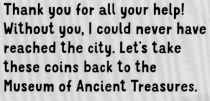

Thank you for all your help! Without you, I could never have reached the city. Let's take these coins back to the Museum of Ancient Treasures.

CODE YOUR OWN KNIGHT ADVENTURE

You receive a note from your old friend Sir Percival. He begs you to meet him at the Great Hall...

Help! Queen Matilda has sent me on a quest. The evil Wizard Malvin has kidnapped her children, Prince George and Princess Georgina, and is holding them prisoner in the Enchanted Castle. Wizard Malvin is the most powerful wizard in the land thanks to his Book of Spells! I need to rescue the prince and princess AND destroy the Book of Spells. P-please, pleeeeease help me with my quest!

Of course you cannot let poor Sir Percival go on his quest alone. But before you set off, you must put on your armor.

KNIGHTTIME

1. Open **Scratch**.

 Let's delete the cat sprite. In the **Sprites Pane**, **right click** the **cat**.

 On a Mac, hold the **"Ctrl"** key then **click**.

Choose **Delete**.

2. To start drawing yourself as a knight, click the **Paint new sprite** button in the **Sprites Pane**.

3. Now you should be able to see the **Drawing Area**.

 Choose the **Ellipse** tool.

 At the bottom of the screen, click the **Solid ellipse**.

4. Select a **skin color**.

Draw your head by dragging the mouse.

5. Choose the **Rectangle** tool.

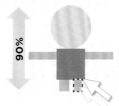

Draw **gray** rectangles for your body, arms, and legs. Your drawing should be **almost as tall** as the Drawing Area. If not, your games might not work.

6. Add more rectangles for your shoes and shield.

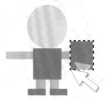

 If things go wrong, click **Undo** and go back a step.

7.  Choose the **Line** tool.

Set it to a **medium thickness**.

8.  Add a belt, sword, and 2 lines at the bottom of your shield.

9. Choose the **Fill** tool then click in your shield.

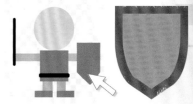

10. Use the **Brush** tool to add details.

 Use the other tools to personalize your outfit.

 Use the **Eraser** to round off your shoes.

Turn the page to find out how to save your knight drawing so you can use it on your quest. Turn over right now!

I think I have an idea! Many years ago, a kind fairy gave me a flying carpet. Surely it could come in handy on our quest! Please help me collect it from my cottage.

FIND THE FLYING CARPET

1. Before you do anything else, save your knight sprite so you can use it in all the other activities in this adventure.

In the **Sprites Pane**, **right click** on the **knight** sprite icon. On a Mac, hold the **"Ctrl"** key and **click**.

Click **Save to local file**.

Type in **knight** as a name for your sprite and click **OK**.

delete

save to local file

2. In the center of the screen, click the **Scripts** tab so Scratch is ready for you to add some code to make your knight move.

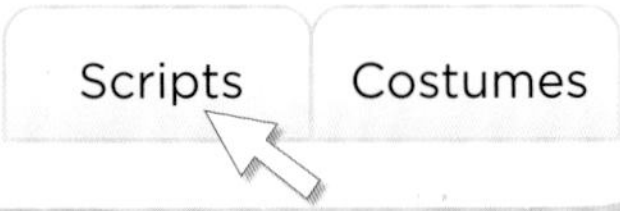

| Scripts | Costumes |

3. Drag these blocks into the **Scripts Area**, in this order. Remember that the color of each block tells us which group it is in. So the **"When green flag clicked"** block is in the **Events** group. The blue blocks are in the **Motion** group. All the purple blocks are in the **Looks** group. The **"Repeat"** loop block is in **Control**. You can click in the white box in a block in order to change the message or number, so click in the **"Say"** block to type in the words.

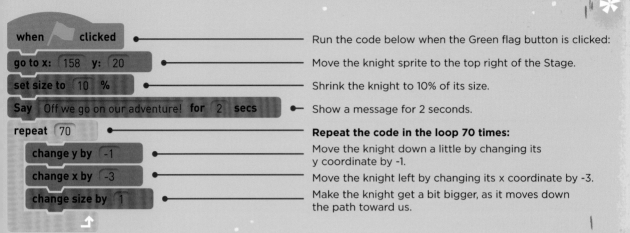

when ▸ clicked	Run the code below when the Green flag button is clicked:
go to x: 158 y: 20	Move the knight sprite to the top right of the Stage.
set size to 10 %	Shrink the knight to 10% of its size.
Say Off we go on our adventure! for 2 secs	Show a message for 2 seconds.
repeat 70	**Repeat the code in the loop 70 times:**
change y by -1	Move the knight down a little by changing its y coordinate by -1.
change x by -3	Move the knight left by changing its x coordinate by -3.
change size by 1	Make the knight get a bit bigger, as it moves down the path toward us.

What are coordinates?

The code above uses coordinates to position and move your knight sprite. If you haven't learned about coordinates in school yet, just try experimenting with different numbers and you'll soon figure it out.

The x number gives Scratch the left to right position on the Stage. The y number gives the top to bottom position.

The position x: 0, y: 0 is in the center of the Stage.

4. Now we will create a backdrop for the Stage to show a path through the forest.

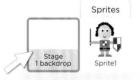

In the **Sprites Pane**, click the **Stage** icon.

Just below, click **Choose backdrop from library**.

Choose **castle3**. Then click **OK**.

5. Click the **Green flag** button at the top right of the **Stage** to test your code. Walk down the path and collect Sir Percival's flying carpet!

To save your code, click the **File** menu, then **Download to your computer**. Then to use it again, click **File** and **Upload from your computer**.

Armed with the flying carpet, you draw near the Enchanted Castle. It lurks at the heart of a very strange forest...

Aaaaargh! These trees are under one of Wizard Malvin's deadly spells!

Leap onto the flying carpet and make your escape from the...

FEARSOME FOREST

1. Start a new Scratch file.

File▼

New

2. In the **Sprites Pane**, **right click** the **cat sprite** icon. On a Mac, hold **"Ctrl"** and **click**.

duplicate

delete

Click **Delete**.

3. In the center of the screen, click **Backdrops**.

Scripts   Backdrops

Choose the **Fill** tool.

Choose **dark green**.

Fill the background by clicking in the **Drawing Area**.

4. Choose the **Brush** tool.

Choose **blue**.

Make the brush width **thicker**.

Draw the castle's moat in the **bottom right corner** of the Drawing Area.

5. Zoom in to make it easier to draw the castle.

400%

Click the **Plus** button to zoom in to **400%**.

6. Use the **scroll bars** to move the backdrop over to the bottom right side.

You need to be able to see the moat.

7. Choose the **Rectangle** tool.

Select **dark gray**, then choose the **Solid rectangle**.

8. Draw the Enchanted Castle inside the moat using rectangles.

Make sure you draw the entrance to the castle in **black**.

9.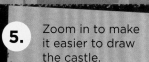

In the **Sprites Pane**, click the **Choose sprite from library** button to add a magic tree.

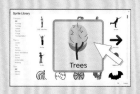

Scroll down then click the **Trees** image.

Click **OK**.

Make sure you use the same tree as this one or your code may not work properly.

10. In the Scratch **Menu bar**, click the **Shrink** button. Now **click** the tree on the **Stage** several times until it is about the same size as the castle.

11. Now upload your **knight** sprite.

In the **Sprites Pane**, click **Upload sprite from file**.

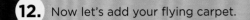

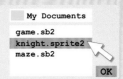

```
   My Documents
game.sb2
knight.sprite2
maze.sb2
                OK
```

Find your file and click **OK**.

The sprite will appear.

Sprite1

12. Now let's add your flying carpet.

Click the **Costumes** tab.

You may have to zoom back to **100%**.

Costumes

🔍 = 🔍 **100%**

Use the **Brush** tool to draw the carpet.

Make the brush **thinner** to draw tassles at each end.

13. Click the **Scripts** tab then drag these blocks into the **Scripts Area**. The **"Touching color"** blocks are in the **Sensing** group. You will need to drop them in the holes in the **"Repeat until"** and **"If then"** blocks.

Scripts

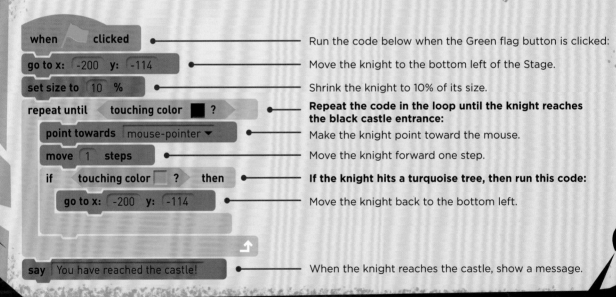

when ▶ clicked — Run the code below when the Green flag button is clicked:

go to x: -200 y: -114 — Move the knight to the bottom left of the Stage.

set size to 10 % — Shrink the knight to 10% of its size.

repeat until touching color ■ ? — **Repeat the code in the loop until the knight reaches the black castle entrance:**

point towards mouse-pointer ▼ — Make the knight point toward the mouse.

move 1 steps — Move the knight forward one step.

if touching color ☐ ? then — **If the knight hits a turquoise tree, then run this code:**

go to x: -200 y: -114 — Move the knight back to the bottom left.

say You have reached the castle! — When the knight reaches the castle, show a message.

How to set the color for a "Touching color" block

Click the colored square.

touching color ☐ ?

The pointer changes.

On the Stage, click the color you want to check for.

The color is now set.

touching color ■ ?

14. Now we'll make more trees.

Right click the tree on the **Stage** and choose **Duplicate**. On a Mac, hold **"Ctrl"** and **click**.

info

duplicate

15. Drag the new tree into a space in the forest.

Repeat step 14 to add more trees, but make sure it's possible for the flying carpet to reach the castle.

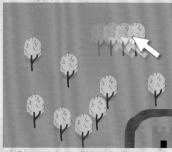

16. Click the **Green flag** button to practice flying around. Move your **mouse pointer** to make the flying carpet sail toward it. Now fly to the castle!

Remember to save your game by clicking the **File** menu, then **Download to your computer**.

Disaster! The Enchanted Castle is protected by a fire-breathing dragon! Can you escape its scorching flames?

DRAGON TROUBLE

1.    Start a new Scratch file and **delete** the **cat sprite**.

2. To create the dragon, click **Choose sprite from library**.

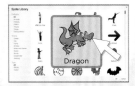 Click the **Dragon** icon.

 OK Click **OK**.

3. Click **Upload sprite from file** to get your **knight** sprite.

 Find your file and click **OK**.

4.  Draw the **flying carpet** again. See page 90 step 12 for help.

5. Click the **Scripts** tab then drag these blocks into the **Scripts Area** to move the **knight**.

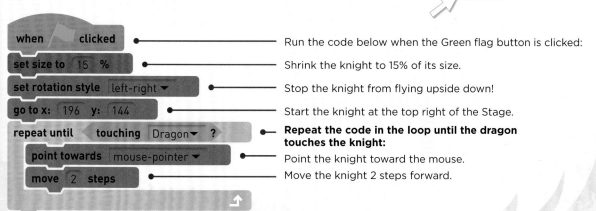

Scripts

when ⚑ clicked — Run the code below when the Green flag button is clicked:

set size to 15 % — Shrink the knight to 15% of its size.

set rotation style left-right ▼ — Stop the knight from flying upside down!

go to x: 196 y: 144 — Start the knight at the top right of the Stage.

repeat until touching Dragon ▼ ? — **Repeat the code in the loop until the dragon touches the knight:**

point towards mouse-pointer ▼ — Point the knight toward the mouse.

move 2 steps — Move the knight 2 steps forward.

6. Now we need to add code to make the dragon move.

Click the **dragon** in the **Sprites Pane**.

Scripts

Click the **Scripts** tab and drag this code into the **Scripts Area**.

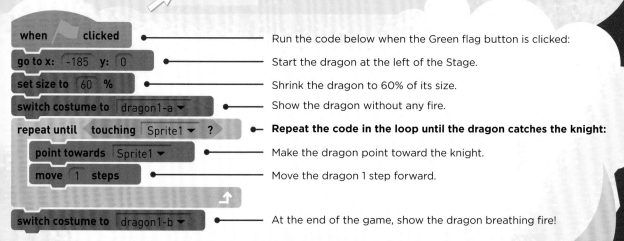

when ⚑ clicked — Run the code below when the Green flag button is clicked:

go to x: -185 y: 0 — Start the dragon at the left of the Stage.

set size to 60 % — Shrink the dragon to 60% of its size.

switch costume to dragon1-a ▼ — Show the dragon without any fire.

repeat until touching Sprite1 ▼ ? — **Repeat the code in the loop until the dragon catches the knight:**

point towards Sprite1 ▼ — Make the dragon point toward the knight.

move 1 steps — Move the dragon 1 step forward.

switch costume to dragon1-b ▼ — At the end of the game, show the dragon breathing fire!

7. Finally, we'll set the backdrop for the Stage to show the outside of the Enchanted Castle.

Click the **Stage** icon.

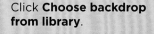

Click **Choose backdrop from library**.

Choose **castle5**. Then click **OK**.

8.  Click the **Green flag** to fly around on the magic carpet. Watch out for those flames!

Don't forget to save your game by clicking **File** then **Download to your computer**.

Escaping the dragon's flames, you land your flying carpet on the battlements. You descend a winding staircase into the gloom of the Enchanted Castle...

Ouch! Eeek! Help! Even the walls are attacking me!

Find Prince George and Princess Georgina quickly! But watch out for the...

ENCHANTED WALLS

1. Start a new Scratch file and **delete** the **cat sprite**.

2. Click the **Backdrops** tab.

Select the **Fill** tool.

Click **light gray**.

Fill in the background by clicking on it.

3. We need to add some walls to the backdrop. (These walls will not move.)

Choose the **Brush** tool and select a **dark gray**.

Make the brush width a little **thicker**.

Draw a small brick outline.

Choose the **Fill** tool and select a **medium gray**.

Fill in the brick wall.

Draw **2** other brick walls in the same way.

When you have finished, your backdrop should look like this, with **3** small brick walls.

4. To add the prince, click the **Choose sprite from library** button.

Prince

Scroll down then click the **Prince** icon.

OK

Click **OK**.

5. Add the princess in the same way.

Princess

Scroll down then click the **Princess**.

OK

Click **OK**.

6. Click the **Shrink** button. Now **click** the **prince** and **princess** several times on the **Stage** until they are the same size as the walls.

7. Drag George and Georgina over to the **right** side of the Stage.

8.

Now upload your **knight** sprite.

Find your file and click **OK**.

9. Click the **Scripts** tab and drag this code to the **Scripts Area** to control the movement of the **knight**. For help with setting the color in the **"Touching color"** block, turn to page 90. All the other light blue blocks are also in the **Sensing** group. Use their drop-down menus to change the key.

Scripts

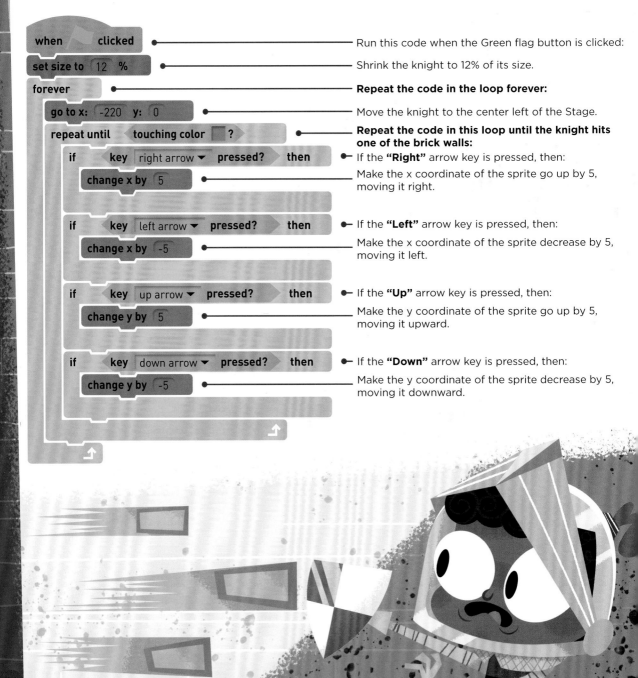

when ⚑ clicked ———— Run this code when the Green flag button is clicked:

set size to 12 % ———— Shrink the knight to 12% of its size.

forever ———— **Repeat the code in the loop forever:**

go to x: -220 y: 0 ———— Move the knight to the center left of the Stage.

repeat until touching color ? ———— **Repeat the code in this loop until the knight hits one of the brick walls:**

if key right arrow ▾ pressed? then ———— If the **"Right"** arrow key is pressed, then:

change x by 5 ———— Make the x coordinate of the sprite go up by 5, moving it right.

if key left arrow ▾ pressed? then ———— If the **"Left"** arrow key is pressed, then:

change x by -5 ———— Make the x coordinate of the sprite decrease by 5, moving it left.

if key up arrow ▾ pressed? then ———— If the **"Up"** arrow key is pressed, then:

change y by 5 ———— Make the y coordinate of the sprite go up by 5, moving it upward.

if key down arrow ▾ pressed? then ———— If the **"Down"** arrow key is pressed, then:

change y by -5 ———— Make the y coordinate of the sprite decrease by 5, moving it downward.

10. Now we'll draw an enchanted wall sprite. It should have about **6 bricks** in it. Leave a **wide gap in the middle** so the knight can fit through.

Click **Paint new sprite**.

When finished, your wall drawing should be **almost the full height** of the Drawing Area. If not, the game might not work properly.

90%

Select the **Brush** and choose **dark gray**.

Draw the outline of **1** brick in the wall.

Draw **2** more bricks below it. Leave a gap, then draw **3** more bricks.

Choose **Fill** and **medium gray**.

Color in the bricks.

11. To make the **enchanted wall** sprite move, click the **Scripts** tab and drag this code to the **Scripts Area**.

Scripts

when ⚑ clicked	Run the code below when the Green flag button is clicked:
set size to 70 %	Shrink the enchanted wall sprite to 70% of its size.
set rotation style don't rotate ▼	Stop the wall from rotating when it changes direction.
point in direction 180 ▼	Start by moving the wall downward.
forever	**Repeat the code in the loop forever:**
if on edge, bounce	If the wall hits the edge of the Stage, bounce it back in the opposite direction.
move 1 steps	Move the wall 1 step in the current direction.

12. Add another wall by **right clicking** the **wall** icon and choosing **Duplicate**.

info

duplicate

13. Drag the new wall into a space. Consider where to position your walls so you don't make the game too hard.

14. Click the **Green flag** to rescue the prince and princess!

Save your game by clicking **File** and **Download to your computer**.

Thank you for coming to rescue us! But you must defeat Wizard Malvin before any of us can escape this castle.

Malvin is hiding in the Dark Tower, guarded by his ghost knights. I kept my magic wand hidden from him. Take it so you can fight his magic with your own!

Sir Percival is shaking with fear! Can you battle the ghost knights and enter the Dark Tower alone?

THE DARK TOWER

1. Start a new file and **delete** the **cat sprite**.

2. Click **Backdrops**.

Scripts | Backdrops

 Choose the **Fill** tool.

 Choose **very dark blue**.

Fill in the background.

3. Choose the **Rectangle** tool.  Select **black**, then click the **Solid rectangle**.

4. Draw the Dark Tower using rectangles.

Start with the base.　　Add the battlements at the top.　　Finish with the grass.

5. Upload your **knight** sprite. Click **Upload sprite from file**.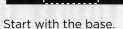

```
My Documents
game.sb2
knight.sprite2
maze.sb2
        OK
```

Find your file and click **OK**.

The sprite will appear.

Sprite1

6. We're going to use the knight quite small, so the sword it's holding will look like Georgina's magic wand! Let's add a flash of magic lightning to fire at the ghost knights from the wand.

Click **Choose sprite from library**.

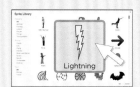

Lightning

Scroll down then click the **Lightning**.

OK

Click **OK**.

7. Click the **Scripts** tab and drag these blocks into the **Scripts Area** for the **lightning** sprite. For the **"Go to sprite1"** block, choose the **"Go to mouse-pointer"** block then use the drop-down menu.

Scripts

when space ▼ key pressed	●—	Run the code below when the **"Space"** key is pressed:
show	●	Make the lightning sprite visible.
set size to 5 %	●	Shrink the lightning to 5% of its size.
go to Sprite1 ▼	●	Move the lightning to the knight sprite.
repeat 20	●	**Repeat the code in the loop 20 times:**
change y by 20	●	Move the lightning up quickly, 20 steps at a time.

8.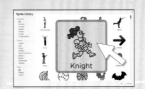

To create a ghost knight, click **Choose sprite from library**.

Scroll down then click the **Knight** icon.

OK

Click **OK**.

9. Click the **Scripts** tab and drag these blocks into the **Scripts Area** for the **ghost knight**. We need to create lots of ghost knights. To do this we will use a special method called cloning, which duplicates sprites when the **"Create clone"** block runs. To make the **"Set ghost effect"** block, drag in a **"Set color effect"** block then use the drop-down menu to change it to **"ghost."**

Scripts

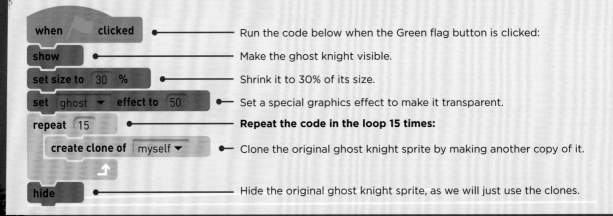

when clicked	Run the code below when the Green flag button is clicked:
show	Make the ghost knight visible.
set size to 30 %	Shrink it to 30% of its size.
set ghost effect to 50	Set a special graphics effect to make it transparent.
repeat 15	**Repeat the code in the loop 15 times:**
create clone of myself	Clone the original ghost knight sprite by making another copy of it.
hide	Hide the original ghost knight sprite, as we will just use the clones.

10. Now we will add code for each **ghost knight** clone. Drag this script **underneath** the code from step 9. It doesn't need to touch any of the previous code. The green **"Pick random"** block is in the **Operators** group. Drop it in the hole in the **"Set x to"** and **"Set y to"** blocks.

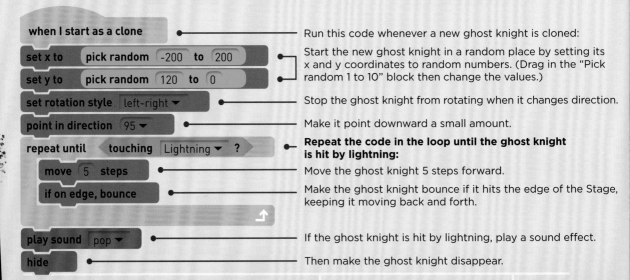

when I start as a clone	Run this code whenever a new ghost knight is cloned:
set x to pick random -200 to 200	Start the new ghost knight in a random place by setting its
set y to pick random 120 to 0	x and y coordinates to random numbers. (Drag in the "Pick random 1 to 10" block then change the values.)
set rotation style left-right	Stop the ghost knight from rotating when it changes direction.
point in direction 95	Make it point downward a small amount.
repeat until touching Lightning ?	**Repeat the code in the loop until the ghost knight is hit by lightning:**
move 5 steps	Move the ghost knight 5 steps forward.
if on edge, bounce	Make the ghost knight bounce if it hits the edge of the Stage, keeping it moving back and forth.
play sound pop	If the ghost knight is hit by lightning, play a sound effect.
hide	Then make the ghost knight disappear.

11. In the **Sprites Pane**, click on your **own knight** sprite. Then drag this code to the **Scripts Area**.

when ⚑ clicked	Run the code below when the Green flag button is clicked:
set size to 12 %	Shrink our own knight to 12% of its size.
go to x: 0 y: -140	Move our knight to the center bottom of the Stage.
wait until touching Knight2 ▼ ?	**Wait until our knight is hit by a ghost knight, then:**
say Agggh! for 2 secs	Show a message.
stop all ▼	Stop all the code from running, because the game is over!

12. Click the **Green flag** to battle with the ghost knights. Press the **"Space"** key to fire your magic lightning bolts at the ghost knights before they reach you and Sir Percival!

Remember to save your game by choosing **File** then **Download to your computer**.

You battle your way into the Dark Tower and come face to face with...WIZARD MALVIN!

HAAAA! So you think you can defeat ME! I have a challenge for you, little knight. Come into the dark woods and battle your magic against mine. If you beat me, I will release the prince and princess —and let you have my Book of Spells. Do you dare fight me?

How can you turn down a challenge like that? Get your magic wand ready!

1. Start a new Scratch file. **Delete** the **cat sprite**.

WIZARD DUEL

2. Let's create a spooky wood background.

Click the **Stage** icon.

Click **Choose backdrop from library**.

Choose **Woods**.

Then click **OK**.

3. To create Wizard Malvin, click **Choose sprite from library**.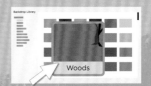

 Scroll down then click the **Wizard** icon.

OK Click **OK**.

4. Now we will add a star sprite from the library (for our magic spells).

Scroll down then click the **Star1** icon.

Click **OK**.

OK

5. Let's also give our knight a magic wand from the library.

Choose the **Magic wand** icon.

Click **OK**.

OK

6. Upload your **knight** sprite.

Click **Upload sprite from file**.

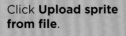
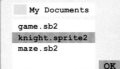

```
My Documents
game.sb2
knight.sprite2
maze.sb2
                    OK
```

Find your file and click **OK**.

The sprite will appear.

7. We will add some code to our **knight** sprite so the game ends if Malvin reaches the knight. Click the **Scripts** tab then drag these blocks into the **Scripts Area**.

Scripts

when ⚑ clicked ●————— Run the code below when the Green flag button is clicked:

set size to 20 % ●————— Shrink the knight to 20% of its size.

wait until touching Wizard ▼ ? ●— **Wait until the knight has been attacked by Wizard Malvin, then:**

say Aggghhh! for 2 secs ●— Show a message.

stop all ▼ ●————— Stop all the code from running, because the game is over!

8. Now we will swap the knight's sword for Georgina's magic wand.

Costumes

In the center of the screen, click the **Costumes** tab.

Use the **Eraser** to rub out the knight's sword.

9.

Click the **Green flag** to run the code. It will make your knight sprite shrink.

Then drag the **knight** sprite over to the **right side** of the Stage by the trees. Drag the **magic wand** sprite onto the knight's arm.

10. In the **Sprites Pane**, click the **magic wand** icon. Click the **Scripts tab**, then drag this code into the **Scripts Area**. It will allow you to move the wand to aim it at Wizard Malvin.

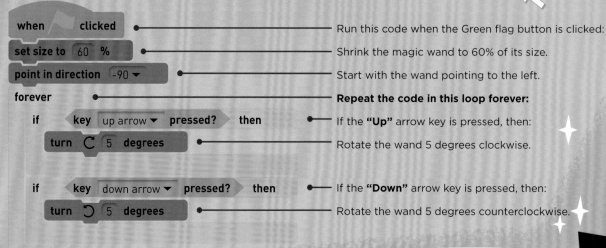

when 🏳 clicked ———————— Run this code when the Green flag button is clicked:

set size to 60 % ———————— Shrink the magic wand to 60% of its size.

point in direction -90 ▼ ———————— Start with the wand pointing to the left.

forever ———————— **Repeat the code in this loop forever:**

if key up arrow ▼ pressed? then ———— If the **"Up"** arrow key is pressed, then:

turn ↻ 5 degrees ———————— Rotate the wand 5 degrees clockwise.

if key down arrow ▼ pressed? then ———— If the **"Down"** arrow key is pressed, then:

turn ↺ 5 degrees ———————— Rotate the wand 5 degrees counterclockwise.

11. In the **Sprites Pane**, click the **star** icon. Drag these two separate chunks of code into the **Scripts Area**. They will control how the spell moves across the screen when you press the "Space" key to cast it.

when 🏳 clicked ———————— Run this code when the Green flag button is clicked:

set size to 25 % ———————— Shrink the star to 25% of its size.

when space ▼ key pressed ———————— When the **"Space"** key is pressed, run this code:

go to Magic Wand ▼ ———————— Move the star to the wand.

point in direction direction ▼ of Magic Wand ▼ ——— Point it in the same direction as the wand.

repeat 30 ———————— **Repeat the code in the loop 30 times:**

move 20 steps ———————— Move the star 20 steps forward.

---

direction ▼ of Magic Wand ▼

Need help finding this code block?

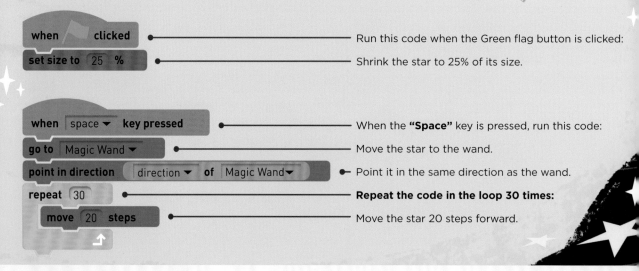

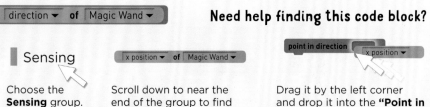

Sensing	x position ▼ of Magic Wand ▼	point in direction x position ▼

Choose the **Sensing** group.

Scroll down to near the end of the group to find this block.

Drag it by the left corner and drop it into the **"Point in direction"** code block.

Choose **Direction**.

Choose **Magic wand**.

12. In the **Sprites Pane**, click the **wizard** icon. Drag these code blocks into the **Scripts Area**.

when [flag] clicked ———— Run this code when the Green flag is clicked:

set size to 70 % ———— Shrink the wizard to 70% of its size.

repeat 20 ———— **Repeat the code in the loop 20 times:**

    go to x: -200 y: pick random -160 to 160 ———— Start the wizard in a random place on the left side of the Stage.

    point towards Sprite1 ▼ ———— Point the wizard toward your knight.

    repeat until touching Star1 ▼ ? ———— **Repeat until the wizard is hit by the spell (star):**

        move 2 steps ———— Move the wizard 2 steps forward.

    change ghost ▼ effect by 5 ———— Make the wizard more transparent each time it is hit.

    play sound pop ▼ ———— Play a sound effect when the wizard is hit.

say You have defeated the wizard! ———— Show a message—your spells have done the job!

13. Use the **arrow keys** on your keyboard to aim, then press the **"Space"** key to fire your spells. Every time you hit Malvin, he will get weaker. Keep going until he disappears!

Don't forget to save your game by choosing **File** then **Download to your computer**.

Aaaaaargh! You are beating me, little knight!

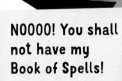

NOOOO! You shall not have my Book of Spells!

Wizard Malvin rips up the Book of Spells before disappearing with a puff of smoke. Quick! Dodge the thunderbolts and pick up all 50 pages of the book.

THE BOOK OF SPELLS

1. Start a new Scratch file and **delete** the **cat sprite**.

duplicate

delete

2. Click **Backdrops**.

Choose the **Fill** tool and pick **dark purple**.

Fill in the background.

3. Now upload your **knight** sprite by clicking **Upload sprite from file**.

4. We need to count how many pages have been collected. We will use a variable. Variables are a way that computer programs store values that can change—such as the score.

Sound
Pen
Data

Click the **Data** group.

Make a Variable

Click **Make a variable**.

Variable name: Pages

Call it **Pages**.

OK

Then click **OK**.

5. To draw a sprite for the thunderbolt, click the **Paint new sprite** button.

The thunderbolt should be about **half the width** of the Drawing Area.

50%

Choose **yellow** and select the **Line** tool.

Make the line **thicker**.

Draw the outline of the thunderbolt.

Choose **Fill** and color in the thunderbolt.

6. Click the **Scripts** tab and drag these blocks into the **Scripts Area** to control the **thunderbolt**.

Scripts

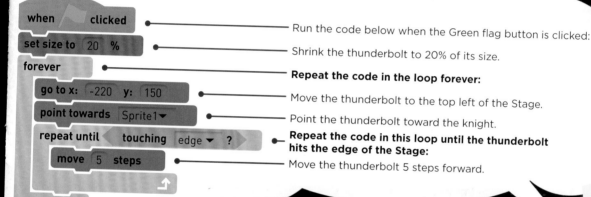

when ⚑ clicked — Run the code below when the Green flag button is clicked:

set size to 20 % — Shrink the thunderbolt to 20% of its size.

forever — **Repeat the code in the loop forever:**

go to x: -220 y: 150 — Move the thunderbolt to the top left of the Stage.

point towards Sprite1 ▼ — Point the thunderbolt toward the knight.

repeat until touching edge ▼ ? — **Repeat the code in this loop until the thunderbolt hits the edge of the Stage:**

move 5 steps — Move the thunderbolt 5 steps forward.

7. In the **Sprites Pane**, click on the **knight** sprite. Then click on the **Scripts** tab and drag these blocks into the **Scripts Area** to control your knight.

Sprite1

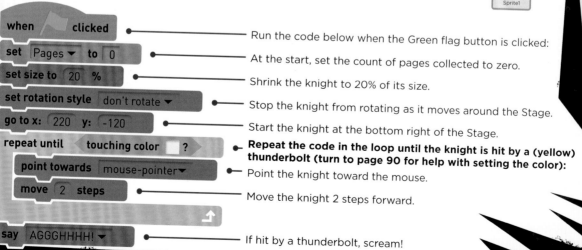

when ⚑ clicked — Run the code below when the Green flag button is clicked:

set Pages ▼ to 0 — At the start, set the count of pages collected to zero.

set size to 20 % — Shrink the knight to 20% of its size.

set rotation style don't rotate ▼ — Stop the knight from rotating as it moves around the Stage.

go to x: 220 y: -120 — Start the knight at the bottom right of the Stage.

repeat until touching color ? — **Repeat the code in the loop until the knight is hit by a (yellow) thunderbolt (turn to page 90 for help with setting the color):**

point towards mouse-pointer ▼ — Point the knight toward the mouse.

move 2 steps — Move the knight 2 steps forward.

say AGGGHHHH! ▼ — If hit by a thunderbolt, scream!

8. Now we will draw a page in the Book of Spells. Click **Paint new sprite**.

The page should be about **half the height** of the Drawing Area.

Frog Spell
Eye of newt,
Hair of dog,
Turn this
creature
Into a frog!

50%

Choose **white** and select the **Rectangle** tool.

Click to draw a **Solid rectangle**.

Draw a rectangle.

Choose **black** and select the **Text** tool.

Click in the rectangle.

Type the spell of your choice.

Frog Spell
Eye of newt,
Hair of dog,
Turn this
creature
Into a frog!

9. Click the **Scripts** tab and drag these two separate chunks of code into the **Scripts Area**. The first one creates 50 cloned pages. The second one tells each cloned page what to do.

Scripts

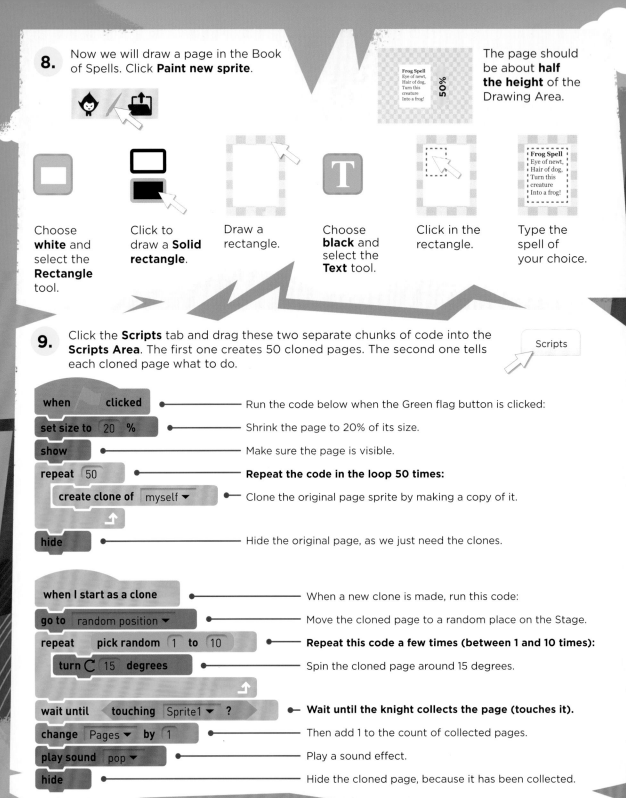

when [ ] clicked — Run the code below when the Green flag button is clicked:

set size to 20 % — Shrink the page to 20% of its size.

show — Make sure the page is visible.

repeat 50 — **Repeat the code in the loop 50 times:**

create clone of myself ▼ — Clone the original page sprite by making a copy of it.

hide — Hide the original page, as we just need the clones.

when I start as a clone — When a new clone is made, run this code:

go to random position ▼ — Move the cloned page to a random place on the Stage.

repeat pick random 1 to 10 — **Repeat this code a few times (between 1 and 10 times):**

turn ↻ 15 degrees — Spin the cloned page around 15 degrees.

wait until touching Sprite1 ▼ ? — **Wait until the knight collects the page (touches it).**

change Pages ▼ by 1 — Then add 1 to the count of collected pages.

play sound pop ▼ — Play a sound effect.

hide — Hide the cloned page, because it has been collected.

10. Now click the **Green flag** button. Move your **mouse pointer** to direct the knight sprite. Watch the score go up as you collect the pages.

Don't forget to save your game!

You can come out now, Sir Percival...

Thank you, kind knight, for rescuing us from Wizard Malvin. Without his Book of Spells he will not be able to cause any more trouble.

GLOSSARY

Animation – A series of pictures shown one after the other to give the illusion of movement (for example, that a sprite is walking).

Clone – One or more copies of a Scratch sprite. Cloning is used to create multiple sprites quickly.

Code – A series of instructions or commands.

Command – A word or code block that tells the computer what to do.

Coordinates – The position of an object determined by its x (center to right) and y (center to top) values.

Data group – The set of Scratch code blocks that control and access variables.

Degree – The unit measuring the angle that an object turns.

Drawing Area – The part of the right-hand side of the Scratch screen that is used to draw sprites and backgrounds.

Duplicate – A simple way to create a copy of a sprite in Scratch.

Events group – The set of Scratch code blocks that are triggered when particular events happen, such as a key being pressed.

If then – A common form of selection in coding, where command(s) are run if something is true.

Language – A system of commands (in the form of blocks, words, or numbers) that tell a computer how to do things.

Loop – A sequence of code blocks repeated a number of times.

Operators group – The set of Scratch code blocks that deals with calculations and comparing values.

Program – The set of commands that tell a computer how to do something such as play a game.

Scratch – A computer language that uses blocks of code to make a program.

Scripts Area – The part of the right-hand side of the Scratch screen to which code blocks are dragged to create programs.

Sensing group – The set of Scratch code blocks that detect when specific keys are pressed or where the mouse is.

Speed – How fast an object moves forward. In Scratch, we use minus speed values to move objects backward.

Sprite – An object that moves around the screen.

Sprites Pane – Part of the lower left of the Scratch screen where you select a sprite to add code to or change its appearance.

Stage – The area at the top left of the Scratch screen where you can watch your sprites move.

Variable – A value or piece of information stored by a computer program. In computer games, a variable is commonly used to store the score.

INDEX

INTERNET SAFETY

Children should be supervised when using the Internet, particularly when using an unfamiliar website for the first time. The publishers and author cannot be held responsible for the content of the websites referred to in this book.

INFORMATION ON RESOURCES

You can use Scratch on a PC or Mac by opening your web browser
and going to: http://scratch.mit.edu
Then click "Try it out."

There is a very similar website called "Snap," which also works on iPads.
It is available here: http://snap.berkeley.edu/run

If you want to run Scratch without using the web, you can download it from here:
http://scratch.mit.edu/scratch2download/

Scratch is developed by the Lifelong Kindergarten Group at MIT Media Lab.
See: http://scratch.mit.edu

Quarto is the authority on a wide range of topics.

Quarto educates, entertains and enriches the lives of our readers—enthusiasts and lovers of hands-on living.

www.quartoknows.com

Author: Max Wainewright
Illustrator: Henry Smith

© 2018 Quarto Publishing plc

First Published in 2018 by QEB Publishing,
an imprint of The Quarto Group.
6 Orchard Road
Suite 100
Lake Forest, CA 92630
T: +1 949 380 7510
F: +1 949 380 7575
www.QuartoKnows.com

A CIP record for this book is available from the Library of Congress.

ISBN 978 1 68297 309 7

Manufactured in Guangdong, China CC042018